FERRARI
FORMULA CARS

FERRARI
FORMULA CARS

GIULIO SCHMIDT

Motorbooks International
Publishers & Wholesalers

This edition first published in 1994 by Motorbooks International Publishers & Wholesalers,
PO Box 2, 729 Prospect Avenue, Osceola, WI 54020 USA
© 1994 Giorgio Nada Editore, Vimodrone (Milan).

Motorbooks International is a certified trademark, registered with the United States Patent Office

The information in this book is true and complete to the best of our knowledge. All
recommendations are made without any guarantee on the part of the author or Publisher,
who also disclaim any liability incurred in connection with the use of this data or specific details

We recognise that some words, model names and designations, for example, mentioned
herein are the property of the trademark holder. We use them for identification purposes only.
This is not an official publication

Motorbooks International books are also available at discounts in bulk quantity for industrial
or sales-promotional use. For details write to Special Sales Manager at the Publisher's address

Library of Congress Cataloging-in Publication Data is Available
ISBN 0 - 87938 - 967 - 2

Printed and bound in Italy.

CONTENTS

PREFACE

"Ferrari cannot live without racing". The emphatic words of Enzo Ferrari liquidate any lingering doubts over the role of a marque such as that of the prancing horse without close contacts with the world of competition. For better or for worse, Ferrari has always played a fundamental role in the general panorama of the Formula 1 World Championship. The Maranello *bolidi* which streak round the world's most prestigious circuits represent veritable symbols of the sport, and F1 would have been hard put to achieve its current degree of success without them.

The Drake always insisted on keeping a close eye on his cars and drivers, at first at the track and then with the passing of the years, increasingly closed in his office "studying" the very last details of the races on television. Ideally this book is dedicated to the Drake himself, to the single-seaters that were designed and "breathed on" by Enzo Ferrari in person. We are thus looking at a gallery of models ranging from the 125 to the F1-87, by way of Alberto Ascari's 500 F2, Phil Hill's 246 F1, Niki Lauda's 312 T and Gilles Villeneuve's 126 C4, all fondly remembered by enthusiasts for their stirring achievements. What follows is rather more than a simple technical catalogue; reading the descriptions of the various models conjours up an idea of the degree of love, passion, tenacity and professionalism that has gone into the Drake's racers.

125 F1

a single stage supercharger. This was the car with which Enzo Ferrari began the "big chase" after Alfa Romeo. The very company which he had served so well, and which he had left in 1939 when the breach between them became an unbridgeable gulf. The split had left some wounds, and a passionate desire for revenge. "I left Alfa—

The race: the Italian Grand Prix at Valentino Park, the 5th of September 1948. The driver: Raymond Sommer. The result: third place. The car: Ferrari 125 F1. The engine: a supercharged 12-cylinder. The story of an enduring legend had just begun. The 125 F1 was the first Grand Prix Ferrari. It dates from 1948, but its story began well before that. At the end of 1946, Ferrari called a press conference at

which he announced his racing programme.
There were to be three models, he said, including sports cars, competition, and Grand Prix versions. The programme, printed on a yellowish paper, bore the signature of the "new Italian car builder".
The sports cars came first, followed by the Grand Prix version. The engine was a 1500 cc 60°V twelve cylinder unit with

Ferrari said one day—because I wanted to show them what I was made of. I knew it was the kind of ambition that can ruin a man." But there were some who helped him.
Such as Gioachino Colombo, the designer of the Alfetta 158, which was the car to beat as a matter of fact. Destiny willed it that Colombo too was at loggerheads with Alfa Romeo in that period.

Maranello came out the loser, even though it was an honourable defeat. In its first world championship Grand Prix, in Monaco, the 125 came second (Ascari) and fourth (Sommer). Then Villoresi came sixth at Spa, while Whitehead was third at Reims. At the Belgian Grand Prix, raced at Spa on the 18th of June 1950, Ferrari introduced a surprise: Alberto Ascari at the wheel of a new car, the 275 with a 12-cylinder 3300 cc aspirated engine. Fangio enjoyed a crushing victory in the Alfa. And yet Ascari's fifth place marked

Gioachino Colombo was the father of the 12-cylinder. He dashed off a sketch of the design

October at the Circuito del Garda during practice for a free formula race. Nino Farina was

on a piece of wrapping paper on the first day of the August holiday of 1945. The technicians who helped transform the design into concrete reality were Giuseppe Busso and above all, Aurelio Lampredi. The 125 F1 made its first appearance at the Italian Grand Prix at the Valentino circuit on the 5th of September 1948. This was the first official clash with the Alfa Romeo. Raymond Sommer managed to take third place, which was a good omen. Success was just around the corner.

It finally arrived on the 24th of

at the wheel. It was an easy win because the Ferrari was the only car of its class in the field. After that the 125 was not seen again until the Swiss Grand Prix of July 3rd 1949 when Alberto Ascari won after a "great race". The victory, all the more emphatic for Gigi Villoresi's second place, was Ferrari's first Formula 1 win. But there were no Alfas at Berne. Nor at Monza, where a modified Ferrari 125 F1 with a two stage supercharger won on its debut on the 11th of September. However, in the head-to-head confrontation with the 8-cylinder Alfa 158,

the beginning of the first serious attack on Alfa's predominance. Aurelio Lampredi's normally aspirated engine was the crucial factor which was to lead to Ferrari's victory over his rivals at Portello within the space of a year. Among the drivers racing with Ferrari in that period, there was Peter Whitehead, the last of the great English gentlemen champions. His car, which can be seen today at the Donington museum, was of the latest generation. It bore chassis number 114. Whitehead had bought it with two engines: a 1500 cc version with single stage supercharger for Formula 1 racing, and a 2 litre unsupercharged motor for Formula 2. He finished nine out of thirteen races with it. He only won one race in the '50-'52 period: the Erlen Grand Prix for F2. In 1954 Whitehead had her fitted with a supercharged 2 litre engine and he went off to race in New Zealand where he won the Lady Wigram Trophy. Then it was sold to Richard Cobden who raced it in Australia and Europe. The V-12 ended up powering a motor boat and it was replaced by a more powerful engine, a 5 litre Chevrolet V-8. Rediscovered in 1973, the original engine was finally remounted back where it belonged.

Engine: front 60° V-12. Displacement: 1496,77 cc. Bore and stroke: 55x52,5 mm. Compression ratio: 6,5:1. Power: 230 bhp at 7000 rpm (1948 version), 260 bhp at 7500 rpm (1949 version), 280 bhp at 8000 rpm (end of 1949). Valve gear: 2 valves per cylinder, sohc (1948), dohc (1949). Fuel system: 1 Weber 50 WCF carburettor, single-stage Roots supercharger (1948), two-stage supercharger (1949). Ignition: single plug, two magnetos. Gearbox: 5 speeds + reverse (1948-'49), 4 speeds + reverse (1950). Brakes: drum. Frame: tubular steel longerons and cross members. Suspension, front: independent, unequal length A-arms, transverse leaf spring, Houdaille hydraulic dampers. Suspension, rear: swing axles, torsion bars, Houdaille hydraulic dampers. In 1950, de Dion axle and longitudinal leaf springs. Tracks: 1255 mm (front), 1200 mm (rear). Wheelbase: 2160 mm (1948), 2320 mm (1950) Weight: 700 kg

166 F2

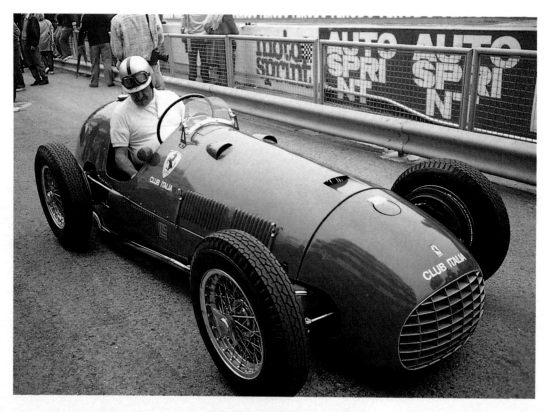

This was the first Formula 2 Ferrari. Derived from the 125 F1. It was also one of the first Formula 2 cars fitted with a 12-cylinder engine. First, it was a sports car disguised as a single-seater. Then, it became a real Formula 2, as from the Florence Grand Prix, the 26th of September 1948. Formula 2 was discussed in the October of 1947 at a meeting of the International Automobile Association in Paris. The regulations required that the engines could not exceed 500 cc if supercharged, and 2000 cc if normally aspirated. Formula 2 races were hybrid affairs for the first part of the 1948 season because no cars has been built specially for that formula yet. The Ferraris and Maseratis were excellent, modern two seaters which were divested of mudguards, lights, spare wheel and occasional seats. The Ferrari F2 was none other than the 166 Inter whose engine had been developed by Aurelio Lampredi up to the 2000 cc ceiling. But just after the 125 F1 underwent its first important test at Turin during the Italian Grand Prix, the real original Ferrari F2 single-seater made its entry at Florence.

Auto Italiana commented: "The brand new Ferrari 2 litre single-seater has finally made its appearance. This clear cut and convincing win makes it safe to say that, if the other marques do not follow Ferrari's example, then this two litre engine of his will have a very easy, not to say too easy, time of it in future competitions."
The win bore the mark of that

great champion Raymond Sommer, who also recorded the fastest lap. The lightened two seater sports were beaten.

The Ferrari F2s were on top in 1949 too. The most prestigious wins were those of Villoresi at Brussels and Rome, and Ascari, who was on his Ferrari debut, at Bari and in the Wimille Cup at Reims, not forgetting Juan Manuel Fangio in the Gran Premio dell'Autodromo di Monza. In the meantime, the 166 F2 had undergone various changes. During 1949 the chassis was lengthened and by the end of 1950 the engine was nearing 310 bhp. Then another five horses were harnessed and the de Dion type rear suspension was adopted. This latter solution, the new rear suspension, had been tried out for the first time on the 10th of April 1950 upon the occasion of the Pau Grand Prix for Formula 1. The car, driven by Ascari, had the four speed box in a unit with the differential, and a lower, sleeker profile. A defective transmission forced Ascari to withdraw before the finish. The car shown in these pages belongs to an Italian collector and it is the 1951 version of the 166 F2. It seems that this is the second model with the de Dion axle to be prepared at Maranello. At Reims on the 2nd of July 1950 Gigi Villoresi subjected it to a test which was as hard as it was unlucky during the Wimille Cup. The car was driven by Dorino Serafini as often as not. The ex European motor cycle champion drove it for

the first time on the 30th of July in a Formula 2 race at Geneva. Both Serafini and Villoresi had cars fitted with de Dion axles and both failed to finish: Serafini had gearbox problems and Villoresi's rear axle broke within sight of the finish. Serafini failed to finish again at the German Grand Prix for Formula 2 at the Nürburgring, while Ascari drove to a prestigious victory. Serafini had started out with the job of keeping the opposition at bay and he was nicely tucked in behind Ascari when the onset of

gearbox trouble had him performing miracles just to stay on the track. The Mettet Grand Prix was just as bad for him but he finally took a place, behind man of the moment Ascari, at the Circuito del Garda on the 15th of October.

Dorino Serafini and his 166 F2 began the 1951 season with a third place in the Grand Prix de Marseilles on the 8th of April, but on the 29th of that same month Serafini went off the road during the Mille Miglia. It was to be the end of his career.

Engine: front 60° V-12. Displacement: 1995,02 cc. Bore and stroke: 60x58,8. Compression ratio: 11:1. Power: 260 bhp at 7000 rpm (1950). Valve gear: 2 valves per cylinder, sohc. Fuel system: atmospheric stet, three carburettors. Ignition: single plug with two magnetos. Gearbox: 5 speeds + reverse, 4 speeds in 1950. Brakes: drum. Frame: tubular with cross members. Suspension, front: independent, unequal length A-arms, transverse leaf spring. Suspension, rear: rigid axle, longitudinal leaf springs (1948). de Dion type (1950). Tracks: in 1950, 1255 mm (front), 1200 mm (rear). Wheelbase: 2420 mm. Weight: 500 kg (dry) in '48; 530 kg in '51.
The data refer to the basic 1948 model.

166 F2

Another model, just as glorious. It is the car with which Alberto Ascari won at the Circuito di Caracalla in 1951 and with which Giannino Marzotto took the Marseilles Grand Prix of the following year. Berardo Taraschi raced it until 1958, taking part in over 18 races.

The 166 series for the Sports class was introduced at the end of 1947. Then, in the April of 1948, a Ferrari advertisement announced the 166 Inter for the international Sport and Racing N. 2 formula, i.e. Formula 2.

The words 166 F2 appeared for the first time in catalogue no. 4 prepared by Ferrari in 1948. Why 166? It's an old question. The number stands for the single piston displacement, rounded up or down. In his book, *Ferrari Story*, Gianni Rogliatti explained: "Through the catalogues it is possible to follow the development of the 166 model in its numerous guises. At first the dimensions of the engine were 60x58, or rather the stroke was the same as the type 159 engine; the real single piston displacement was just short of 166 cc and the overall displacement was shown as 1992 cc. In the 1948 catalogue (the one showing the four versions: Sport, Inter, Mille Miglia and F2) the new stroke is given as 58.8 mm, the single piston displacement as 166.25 cc and the overall displacement as 1995 cc. These elements were to remain unchanged". The official debut of the 166 F2, as a single-seater specially

conceived for the new Formula, took place at the Florence Grand Prix on the 26th of September 1948. But it had already taken part, without fanfare, in a race at Perpignan on the 25th of April where Sommer took a good third place. Corrado Millanta, writing in the pages of *Auto Italiana*, explained that the car was a successful marriage between the new supercharged Grand Prix Ferrari and the

Ferrari sport, whose engine it had received. "Naturally this

engine is more 'highly strung' than the one its creator calls the "Mille Miglia" version. They say it produces 155 bhp at 7000 rpm, the equivalent of 78

Engine: front 60° V-12. Displacement: 1995,02 cc. Bore and stroke: 60x58,8 mm. Compression ratio: 11:1. Power: 160 bhp at 7000 rpm (1950). Valve gear: 2 valves per cylinder, sohc. Fuel system: atmospheric induction, three carburettors. Ignition: single plug with two magnetos. Gearbox: 5 speeds + reverse, 4 speeds in 1950. Brakes: drum. Frame: tubular, with cross members. Suspension, front: independent, unequal length A-arms, transverse leaf spring. Suspension, rear: rigid axle, longitudinal leaf springs (1948). de Dion type (1950). Tracks: in 1950 1225 mm (front), 1200 mm (rear). Wheelbase: 2160 mm, 2320 mm (1949). Weight: 550 kg (dry) in 1948; 530 kg in 1951. The data refer to the 1948 model.

horsepower per litre. Thanks to the high fractionization of the displacement and the bore/stroke ratio being less than unity (the stroke is only 58.9 mm), the linear velocity of the piston is kept within a good safety margin (13.8 metres a second) for a racing car. This engine with 12 cylinders disposed along two banks and set in a V is fitted with three down draft twin carburettors.

Not many people know that—given the unusual distance between the cylinder axes, due in turn to the fact that the con rods on the crank pin were not forked but side by side—it was possible to use hairpin springs for the valve return action (just like those used in most motor cycle engines). These are better than the cylindrical type because being further away from the column of gas they work in a

cooler environment. The tubular chassis, has the axle fixed to the frame, self locking differential and swing axles. The front suspension was the torsion bar type. Weight: 550 kg. Given the power of the 155 bhp we are talking about 3.5 kg per unit of horse power." Millanta's description is very detailed and it gives an idea of the importance which the Italian press gave to the car's official introduction.

Also of note was the degree of "feedback" between the 166 F2 and the 125 F1. At first the 166 F2 was the fruit of experience gained with the 125 F1, then it became an experimental car itself, thanks to a lower chassis which lent it stability and manoeuverability.

It took part in thirteen races and won six of them in the 1949 season. Things went even better

the following season: seventeen races, thirteen wins.

The model shown in these pages belongs to the last generation of the 166 F2. Ferrari sold it to Giannino Marzotto on the 14th of July 1951. Marzotto then sold it to Berardo Taraschi on the 13th of August 1954.

Alberto Ascari won at the Circuito di Caracalla driving this model in 1951 while Marzotto won at Marseilles in 1952. Taraschi drove the car from 1954 to 1958 taking part in over 18 races in which he obtained good placings.

In the meantime the new Ferrari F2 had arrived. Aurelio Lampredi's four cylinder car made its first appearance on the test track at Modena on the 23rd of May 1951 driven by Gigi Villoresi.

212 F1

A special model for 1951. A twelve cylinder engine derived from the sports cars. Formula 2 frame. Aurelio Lampredi, the designer, was already thinking of the future Formula 1 which called for unsupercharged engines of up to 2500 cc as from 1954. Debut at the Siracusa Grand Prix, 11th March 1951.

Ferrari had no rivals in Formula 2. But in Formula 1, despite evident progress, they still had to beat Alfa Romeo. And yet the Ferrari technicians led by Aurelio Lampredi were already thinking about the Formula for 1954 which imposed a maximum displacement of 2500 cc for

normally aspirated engines. In 1951 therefore Ferrari introduced the 212, a special F1 model, obtained by mounting a larger engine derived from those produced for the Sports cars onto a typical F2 chassis. This was still a 2563 cc V12 engine with the cylinders at 60 degrees which produced 200 hp at 7500 rpm. When it appeared for the first time in Sicily at the Siracusa Grand Prix on the 11th March 1951, the 212 was a real surprise. This was also because there were two models. The first, driven by Dorino Serafini,

had the 166 F2 chassis with the de Dion axle and the 2562 cc 12-cylinder engine. The second, driven by the Swiss, Rudolf Fischer, in the colours of the new Espadon stable, had a conventional chassis and independent rear suspension. Gigi Villoresi, back at the track after the terrible accident at Geneva, and Alberto Ascari both drove the unsupercharged "4500"s at Siracusa. These were the same ones which had raced the year before at Monza and Barcellona. The debut of the new 4500s with twin plug ignition was also expected, but

Ferrari preferred to play his cards close to his chest for a while yet, largely because Alfa Romeo had sent no cars to Sicily. Villoresi won while Ascari failed to finish.

The success of the 4500 went without saying. Louveau and Rosier in the Talbots could do little about it. Technical interest was concentrated entirely on the new Ferrari 2500s and they were no disappointment. Dorino Serafini came second and Rudolf Fischer third. *Auto Italiana* commented: "With the new 2500 cc, Ferrari has now got a car which corresponds to Formula 1954. Naturally this is a classic 12-cylinder Ferrari with three carburettors which produces about 180 bhp for the moment: another product from the indefatigable Lampredi, now head of design at Ferrari and the man to whom we owe the victorious 4500s." Some well earned recognition for the ebullient engineer from Tuscany who was no longer under the supervision of Gioachini Colombo, who had moved to Maserati.

But the 212 F1 performed poorly at the Pau Grand Prix of the 26th of March. Serafini failed to finish and Fischer could only manage sixth. By way of consolation, Ferrari could point to Villoresi's win in

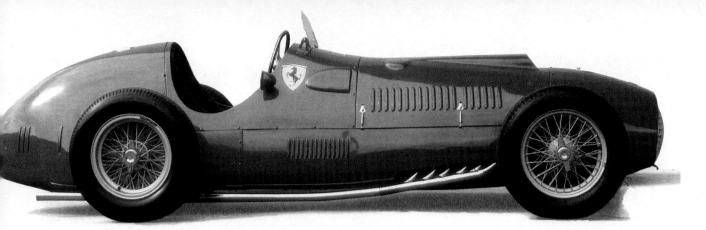

the 1950 version of the 375. It was to be Serafini's last race in the 212 F1 and Fischer drove it in the races which followed. The Swiss surprised everybody at the San Remo GP on the 22nd of April when he took third place. Seven days later in Bordeaux he even came second, only to come a poor eleventh on the Brema circuit in the Swiss Grand Prix. Technical problems? No, his goggles steamed up. Then he came fourth in Holland, on the 22nd of July. Sixth in Germany, the 29th of July. Fischer drove the same car with good results in 1952: third in the Turin Grand Prix on the 6th of April and sixth at Albi on the 1st of June. The car shown in these pages, now owned by an Italian collector, is the 212 F1 which Dorino Serafini raced at the Siracusa and Pau Grand Prix of 1951.

Engine: front 60° V-12. Displacement: 2562,51 cc. Bore and stroke: 68x58,8 mm. Compression ratio: 12:1. Power: 200 bhp at 7500 rpm. Valve gear: 2 valves per cylinder, sohc. Fuel system: atmospheric induction, three carburettors. Ignition: single plug with two magnetos. Gearbox: 4 speeds in a unit with the differential, 5 speeds in unit with the engine. Brakes: drum. Frame: tubular, with cross members. Suspension, front: unequal length A-arms, transverse leaf springs, hydraulic dampers. Suspension, rear: de Dion axle. Tracks: 1225 mm (front), 1250 mm (rear). Wheelbase: 2320 mm. Weight: 600 kg.

375 F1

have to increase the displacement gradually when working with a basic design. And so the first version was known as the 275 according to the usual rule of single piston displacement. It had a bore and stroke of 72x68 mm, the con rod was 142 mm long, single piston displacement was 276.8 cc and overall displacement 3322 cc.

The most celebrated of the cars with Lampredi's unsupercharged 12-cylinder engine. It took Ferrari to the heights of Formula 1 in 1951, after a famous victory at the British Grand Prix at Silverstone in which Alfa Romeo was beaten for the first time. This was the weapon Enzo Ferrari used to take "revenge" on Alfa Romeo. The Modena constructor had realized by this time that the supercharger no longer represented the pathway to success. Towards the end of the 1950 season, Ferrari introduced his new normally aspirated 12-cylinder engine. It bore the signature of Aurelio Lampredi, "the most prolific designer I ever had", as Ferrari

said of him. "The engine—wrote Gianni Rogliatti in *Ferrari Story*—came out smaller than the definitive version in accordance with a reliable rule of thumb which says that you

Power was initially 260 bhp at 7000 rpm."
This engine made its Formula 1 debut at the Belgian Grand Prix raced at Spa on the 18th of June 1950. The frame was

substantially the same as that of the supercharged 125, which had to remain in harness until the definitive launch of the new normally aspirated unit. The experimental phase is encapsulated in these results: Ascari was fifth in Belgium, Villoresi failed to get underway in the French Grand Prix and failed to finish at Albi. On the 30th July, in the Grand Prix des Nations at Geneva, Ferrari introduced two cars with the type 340 engine, i.e. with displacement increased to 4102 cc and output upgraded to 320 bhp.

"During the night—wrote Corrado Millanta in *Auto Italiana*—the Ferrari transporters arrived full of new goodies. Along with the 275 F1, which if it wasn't exactly a novelty was still something relatively new,

there were two new single-seaters which attracted swarms of technicians. There was no accompanying official declaration giving technical specifications, but one knew intuitively that this was the next step in the development of the aspirated single-seater. Some maintained that we were in the presence of the definitive version, which had already been taken to the 4500 cc limit, alias

the 375 F1. Bazzi and Lampredi, beseiged with questions, said that, as they had still to measure the bore they didn't know the exact displacement! This was really the 4100 cc type 340 F1, the intermediate stage between the 3,300 and the maximum permitted limit of 4.5 liters." The race turned out to be dramatic. Villoresi ploughed into the crowd and several spectators

Engine: front 60° V-12. Displacement: 4493,73 cc. Bore and stroke: 80x74,5 mm. Compression ratio: 11:1. Power: 350 bhp at 7000 rpm. Valve gear: 2 valves per cylinder, sohc. Fuel system: atmospheric induction, three carburettors. Ignition: single plug with 2 magnetos, twin plug with 1 magneto (1951). Gearbox: 4 speeds + reverse in unit with the differential. Brakes: hydraulic drum. Frame: tubular, with rectangular side members. Suspension, front: independent, unequal length A-arms, transverse leaf spring, Houdaille Hydraulic dampers. Suspension, rear: de Dion axle, transverse leaf springs, hydraulic dampers. Tracks: 1278 mm (front), 1250 mm (rear). Wheelbase: 2320 mm; 2420 mm (1951). Weight: 850 kg (dry).

were killed. The Milanese driver was severely injured. Then Ascari withdrew leaving the road clear for the `Alfisti' who took the first three places with Fangio, de Graffenried and Taruffi. The disappointment was tangible at Ferrari.

Finally, on the 3rd of September, the 375 F1 with the 4494 cc engine and single piston displacement of 374.4 cc made its debut at Monza. It was the single plug version. That is: one spark plug per cylinder. There were two cars: one for Ascari, the other for Serafini. Their task was no simple one. They had to take on the new Alfa 159s, driven by Fangio and Farina, and the glorious 158s with Taruffi, Fagioli and Sanesi. A furious battle got underway right from practice between Fangio, the fastest, and Ascari, who gave him a mere tenth of a second. The race was up to expectations. Ascari was in the lead for laps 14 and 15 but seven laps later the Milanese had to surrender. Serafini held on well though, and when he made a fuel stop the car was handed over to Ascari who got to the finish in second place. Alfa Romeo had won yet again and Farina was world champion. But that second place for Serafini-Ascari was universally interpreted as the birth of a new era in Formula 1. The car shown in these pages is a single plug type 375 F1. According to the owner, a Dutch collector, the chassis is the one which raced in the 1950 Swiss Grand Prix with the 340 engine and then at Monza with the 4500 cc version driven by Ascari or as is more likely, by Serafini. If so, it would be the car which came second that day.

375 F1

The twin plug version. Its story began on the 22nd April 1951, at the Ospedaletti circuit at San Remo. A win, with Alberto Ascari. It was less successful than the "single plug" version. Froilan Gonzalez had a win at Pescara. Then triumph at the Italian Grand Prix (Monza) with Alberto Ascari. During 1951, the single plug 375 continued racing while the version with 24 spark plugs also made its appearance. It is not hard to tell the difference. In the "single plug" the spaces between the exhausts are equal; in the "twin plug" they are irregular. The "single plug" carried off the most prestigious wins. After the Monza debut, towards the end of 1950, the 375 clinched its first success in the Barcelona Grand Prix, at the Penya Rhin circuit. A hat trick: Ascari, Serafini and Taruffi, the latter in the 340 version. Alfa was not present. But the new 1500 cc, 16 cylinder supercharged BRM was soundly beaten.

The 375 F1 took part in the first three races of the 1951 season, none of which was valid for the world championship. Villoresi won at Siracusa and Pau and Serafini was second at San Remo. In the world championship, Villoresi failed to finish in Switzerland and Taruffi did likewise in Belgium. Then Froilan Gonzalez took a single plug 375 F1 round Silverstone faster than anybody else to give

Ferrari its first world championship win, and the first triumph over the arch rivals at Alfa Romeo. It is a historic date: the 14th July 1951. Fifteen days later victory followed when Ascari conquered the Nurburgring circuit. The story of the twin plug 375 (two spark plugs per cylinder) began with a victory at the Ospedaletti circuit on the 22nd of April 1951 in the San Remo Grand Prix. Alberto Ascari was at the wheel. The win at San Remo seemed to be the harbinger of great things for the new 375, but it wasn't to turn out that way. Ascari had to be content with sixth place at the first world championship test at Berne. Things went better at Spa, with Ascari second and Villoresi third. This result was repeated at Reims. On the day of Gonzalez' triumph in the "single plug" car at Silverstone, Villoresi was third and Ascari withdrew. At the Nurburgring, where Ascari won in the "single plug" 375, Gonzalez was second, Villoresi third and

Taruffi fourth. The "twin plug" 375 rediscovered its winning ways with Gonzalez in the Pescara Grand Prix. The Argentinian came second in the Bari Grand Prix; Ascari and Villoresi failed to finish. Ferrari presented four 375s at Monza on the 16th of September: three were new, driven by Ascari, Villoresi and Gonzalez; Taruffi drove an older model. Ascari headed a crushing Ferrari victory: Gonzalez was second, Villoresi fourth and Taruffi fifth. A pitiless public booed Alfa Romeo. Alfa Romeo took revenge in Spain where Fangio and Ascari were battling it out for the world title. It was a "black" Sunday for Ferrari. Ascari's tyres betrayed him one after the other and with them went his hopes of taking the world title from Fangio. However, Gonzalez was second, Ascari fourth, while Villoresi and Taruffi failed to finish.

The car shown in these pages is the twin plug version. According to Victor J. Pigott, it is the same one which Ascari drove at Monza and Barcelona. It was sold to a Brazilian, Chico Landi, in 1952. It was raced at Priapolis in Uruguay and then at Silverstone, Boreham and Albi. It took part in other races between 1952 and 1954 and was rediscovered in Brazil at the beginning of the '70s.

Engine: front 60° V-12. Displacement: 4493,73 cc. Bore and stroke: 80x74,5 mm. Compression ratio: 11:1. Power: 380 bhp at 7000 rpm (beginning 1951), 385 bhp (end 1951). Valve gear: 2 valves per cylinder, sohc. Fuel system: atmospheric induction, three twin carburettors. Ignition: twin plug, with one magneto (1951). Gearbox: 4 speeds + reverse in unit with the differential. Brakes: hydraulic drum. Frame: tubular, with rectangular side members. Suspension, front: independent, unequal length A-arms, transverse leaf spring, Houdaille hydraulic dampers. Suspension, rear: de Dion axle, transverse leaf spring, hydraulic dampers. Tracks: 1278 mm (front), 1250 mm (rear). Wheelbase: 2320 mm; 2420 mm (1951). Weight: 850 kg (dry).

500 F2

"Racing cars," said Enzo Ferrari, "are neither beautiful nor ugly. They become beautiful when they win." By this reckoning the 500 was gorgeous. It might have lacked the musicality of other Ferraris, but it certainly was not found wanting as far as a winning habit was concerned - an all important quality for a racing car. It was a habit so deeply ingrained that she completed two hard fought seasons virtually unbeaten, and this in the years in which races were staged almost every Sunday at a relentless rhythm throughout Europe.
Ferrari was faced with the challenge mounted by the strongest teams of the era led by Maserati, the British HWM and Connaughts, the competitive Gordinis and myriad cars from minor constructors all keen to have a tilt at the all-conquering Ferraris. The 500 failed to bring home the laurels on just a couple of occasions, carried Ascari to two world titles, guaranteed the fame of Enzo Ferrari and Lampredi and was the pride and joy of numerous private entrants who found the powerful, versatile and easy-to-run machine ideally suited to their needs. The 500 was perhaps the most successful Ferrari racer and it was certainly the simplest. Its simplicity was actually its strongest suit, the factor which made it invincible on all circuits.

Ingegnere Lampredi who had moved to Ferrari from the aeronautics firm Officine Reggiane judged twelve cylinders to be an unnecessary complication in a 2-litre car, firmly suggesting that four would be the ideal number. Enzo Ferrari was initially sceptical, but once convinced that there was something to the idea he did not hesitate in encouraging, motivating and finally supporting him as only Ferrari, that "great mover of men" knew how. On 23 September, 1951, three months after pen was first put to paper on the drawing board, two Ferrari 2-litre F2 cars equipped with the new four-cylinder engine made their debuts at the Modena Grand Prix. The reasoning behind Enzo Ferrari's decision to launch the car in the junior formula reflected his crystalline logic and grasp of practicalities. His naturally aspirated 4500 had achieved a number of victories in F1, but Alfa was still going strong and Formula 1 was too expensive. What was needed was a means of winning immediately, winning everything and, if possible, winning without spending too much money. Why leave all the Formula 2 glory to Maserati and Gordini?
Lampredi was the right man in the right place. His engine, with its total displacement of

1984,859 cc, was already producing 170 hp at 7200 rpm at the Modena Grand Prix. The 500's chassis design was derived from that of the 4500 F1 machine and was based on two oval longerons reinforced by cross members. The front suspension was fully independent whilst at the rear a freely interpreted de Dion layout was adopted with Lampredi adding two longitudinal thrust and reaction arms. The bodywork for the Modena debut was also inspired by the 4500. The new F2 car displayed its potential immediately with Ascari winning at an average speed of over 116 kph.

At the end of the year Lady Luck dealt a winning hand to Enzo Ferrari: Alfa Romeo announced its retirement from racing, Formula 1 went into an immediate decline and the race organizers, left to choose between F1 and F2 for the World Championship races, plumped en masse for F2. Ferrari thus found himself in the happy position of being able to tackle the 1952 Championship on what were virtually his own terms and with tried and trusted machinery. Over the winter the bodywork of the Modena-winning 500 was simplified, uprated brakes were fitted along with a new fuel system featuring four Weber DOE 45 single-barrel carburettors. Further modifications were made to the state of tune and the camshafts. The revised 500 with Ascari at the wheel made a winning debut at Siracusa. This race was a non-championship event, as were the next two at Pau and Marseilles. Ascari won again in France whilst at the successive Naples Grand Prix it was Farina's 500 that took the

honours. In the meantime slight modifications were made to the exhaust system with the adoption of the so-called "organ-pipes".

Following the preliminary races, the first World Championship round was held on 18 May at Bern. On this occasion the works Ferrari F2's ran with fine mesh radiator grilles with lower panels. Taruffi won in front of Fischer's privately entered 500. Farina and Simon's cars were penalized by overheating magnetos.

Villoresi had also suffered from similar problems in earlier races due to the location of the magnetos behind the engine. On 8 June the G.P. dell'Autodromo was held at Monza in conjunction with the drawing of the Monza lottery. The works 500's featured a new front air intake and a more tapered nose without a radiator

grille. The race was run over two legs and was extremely closely fought due to the excellent showing put up by the Maseratis. Overall victory went to Farina after a thrilling, incident packed contest. With races following one after another at a remarkable rate, two weeks after Monza the works 500's of Ascari, Farina and Taruffi lined up for the European Grand Prix on 22 June at

Spa. As had become the norm over the last few races there were also a number of privately entered 500's at the Belgian track. The three works Ferrari again featured modifications: they had lost weight and had small deflector tabs behind the front wheels; Ascari's car also had two small slots in the tail to provide cooling for the oil tank and the transmission. Ascari won again, proving to be the most positive member of the team. A week later, on 29 June at Reims, the Ferrari 500 suffered its first defeat. The race was dominated by a brilliant Jean Behra driving a six-cylinder Gordini whilst Ascari and Villoresi were sidelined by the usual problems with overheating magnetos. The works Ferraris were modified at record breaking speed in time for the Rouen Grand Prix on 6 July

with a definitive solution to the problem being found.

Ascari, Farina and Taruffi's 500s with the new magneto arrangement confirmed their superiority with a magnificent 1-2-3 at Silverstone on the occasion of the British Grand Prix on 19 July. The works Ferraris of Ascari, Farina and Taruffi were joined by the privately entered 500's of the Swiss driver Fischer and the Englishmen Salvadori and Whitehead. Blasting away from the line, Ascari led from start to finish and won at an average speed of 146.290 kph. Little more than two weeks later, just enough time to transfer from Great Britain to Germany, the Ferraris were on the track once more for the German Grand Prix at the demanding Nürburgring circuit on 3 August. All three cars featured modified transverse leaf spring shackles. The race was fascinating, hard fought with Ascari leading home a Ferrari quartet. This was the increasingly popular "Ciccio" Ascari's third victory at the German circuit and he was thus crowned King of the Nürburgring. Following the team's triumphs in Germany Ascari again dominated at the Dutch Grand Prix at Zandvoort on 17 August. Farina and Villoresi were second and third. Ascari took part in two races in France in August, at Saint Gaudens and at La Baule. Thanks to the points accumulated in the earlier races he conquered the French national championship well before the world title.

On 7 September at the Italian Grand Prix at Monza Ascari went into the decisive World Championship round as favourite for outright victory. The

Ferrari team was present in force to support him. There were five works cars driven by Ascari himself, Farina, Villoresi, Taruffi and Simon, as well as five privateers, Rosier, Fischer, De Tornaco, Stuck and Whitehead. With 10 Ferraris in the running it was always going to be difficult for any other marque, but Bonetto and Gonzales with the Maseratis came close to ruining the party and it needed a flash of genius by Ascari to take the chequered flag ahead of Gonzales in the Maserati, the Ferraris of Villoresi and Farina and the Maserati of Bonetto. At Modena on 14 September Maserati was out for

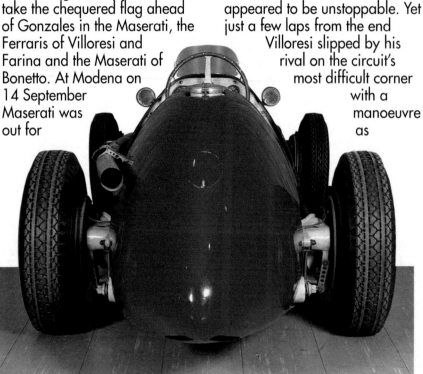

revenge. Things were looking good for the team when the Ferraris of Ascari and Farina both retired with mechanical problems. Villoresi was still in the running for Ferrari but

Gonzales in the Maserati appeared to be unstoppable. Yet just a few laps from the end Villoresi slipped by his rival on the circuit's most difficult corner with a manoeuvre as audacious as it was unexpected. Another victory for the 500 wrapped up a year in which it proved victorious in all the races in which it started with the exception of Reims. The

magnificent Ascari took the World Championship as well as the French national title.

In 1953 the 500 was to be the car to beat. Few modifications were made over the winter as you do not meddle with a winning car. The first race of the new season was the Argentine Grand Prix held on 18 January at the new 12 de Octubre circuit at Buenos Aires. Ferrari entrusted its four works 500s to Ascari, Villoresi, Farina and its new signing Hawthorn. The cars featured a longer nose section and larger 7.00x16 rear tyres. There was a fierce battle with the Maseratis driven by Fangio and Gonzales on their home ground. Ascari won but Farina's accident in which 9 people lost their lives cast a dark shadow over the event.

The second outing of the season saw the 500 suffer the most remarkable defeat of its career: all the works cars retired with broken valve springs. However, at the Pau Grand Prix on 6 April the Ferraris were back in winning form. Once again Ascari led the pack home, with Hawthorn second and Rosier fifth. At Bordeaux on 3 May the Ferraris of Ascari, Villoresi and Farina easily repelled the attacks of the Gordinis driven by Fangio, Schell and Trintignant. Ascari won again ahead of

Engine: front-mounted in-line four-cylinder. Displacement: 1984.85 cc. Bore and Stroke: 90x78 mm. Compression ratio: 13:1. Max. power: 185 hp at 7500 rpm. Valve gear: twin overhead camshafts, two valves per cylinder. Fuel system: two Weber 50 DCO or four Weber 45 DOE carburettors. Ignition: twin magnetos. Gearbox: 4-speed + reverse. Brakes: hydraulically actuated drums. Chassis: tubular longerons and cross members. Suspension, front: independent, wishbones, lower transverse leaf spring. Suspension, rear : de Dion axle, transverse leaf spring. Track: 1270 mm (front), 1250 mm (rear). Wheelbase: 2160 mm. Weight: 560 kg.

Villoresi.

Hawthorn driving the sole works Ferrari won at Silverstone, whilst on 17 June at the championship round at Zandvoort Ferrari was represented by Ascari, Villoresi, Farina and Hawthorn as well as the privateer Rosier. Victory went to Ascari with Farina second, Hawthorn fourth and Rosier seventh. Little changed at the Belgian Grand Prix at Spa, Ascari winning ahead of Villoresi with Hawthorn sixth. Farina retired with a broken engine.

At Reims on 5 July Ferrari won yet again, this time with Hawthorn taking the honours. The Englishman soon repeated his success in the non-championship Ulster Grand Prix. Ascari won the next championship round, the British Grand Prix at Silverstone, and staked a firm claim to his second successive world title. The German Grand Prix was a veritable triumph for Ferrari. On that occasion the cars were fitted with Weber 50 DCO twin-barrel carburettors with a vibration damping rubber coupling. Power output rose to 185 hp at 7500 rpm. Farina came home first after a thrilling battle with Fangio. The Argentine was second in the Maserati with Hawthorn third. Ascari lost a wheel during the race but

finished eighth after taking over Villoresi's car.

The Swiss Grand Prix was held at Bern on the Bremgarten circuit on 23 August. There was another heated battle between the Maseratis of Bonetto, Fangio, Marimon and De Graffenried and the Ferraris driven by Ascari, Villoresi, Farina and Hawthorn. For this race the Ferraris were fitted with 5.25x16 front and 6.50x16 rear tyres. Ascari won the race and was thus mathematically certain of taking the World Championship for the second year running. At the Italian Grand Prix on 13 September Ferrari entered the same cars along with the new "Squalo" or "Shark" with a four-cylinder undersquare engine, a space

frame chassis and lateral fuel tanks. The works 500's were driven by Ascari, Farina, Villoresi and Hawthorn. Carini and Maglioli drove the two Squalos. The race became part of Grand Prix legend thanks to the competitiveness demonstrated by all the drivers. Fangio's Maserati and the Ferraris of Ascari and Farina were all in with a chance of victory up until the last lap. Ascari followed by Farina was in the lead going into the banked corner but spun to avoid a back marker. Fangio found a way through the confusion and went on to win. This brought the 500's season to an end and Ferrari was left to celebrate its second World Championship conquered with its F2 cars.

555 F1
SUPERSQUALO

The 553 was a "shark" the 555 was a "Supershark" on account of the two lateral tanks. Debut at Bordeaux in 1955. Last world title race: Argentine Grand Prix of '56. The end of Aurelio Lampredi's four in line engine. He left Ferrari.
We find the 375 again under the skin of Vandervell's "Thin Wall", driven by Reginald Parnell what's more. It was with an Indy version of the 375 that Alberto Ascari tried to conquer Indianapolis in 1952. He managed to qualify and started in the ninth row. He fought his way up to eighth place but then the hub of the right hand side rear wheel gave way taking Ferrari's American dream along with it. But there was a consolation in store for the Modena car builder that year: Alberto Ascari drove the 500 F2 to the first world title.
The feat was repeated the following season. These were the years in which the world championship was a Formula 2 affair. The Ferrari 500 had no peer. It was the car with the highly successful four cylinder engine designed by Aurelio Lampredi; the car which won more Grand Prix races than any other for Ferrari.
The new Formula 1 came into force in 1954. Cars with aspirated engines could have a maximum displacement of 2500 cc and those with a supercharger, 750 cc. There were no limits on weight or fuel.
In 1953 the first photo of a new car appeared in the pages of *Auto Italiana*. This was the 553 with a two litre, four cylinder engine. It had different lines from the 500. Lower coachwork and a reinforced frame. The two laterally mounted fuel tanks gave it the look of a "squalo", or shark.
Two cars of this type were entered for the Italian Grand

Prix at Monza. Maglioli came eighth, four laps behind Fangio in the Maserati.

Carini did not finish. Enzo Ferrari let it be known that he might well quit racing if some economic help for the "small constructors" was not forthcoming. And in fact Mercedes was coming. This was tantamount to saying: organization, money and technology. However, Ferrari gritted his teeth and entered the F1 world championship with two types of car: the 625 (which had made its debut with Taruffi in the 1951 Bari Grand Prix)

and the '553'.

The F1 version of the "Shark" with the 2.5 litre engine lined up for its first G.P. outing at Siracusa in 1954 with Froilan Gonzalez at the wheel. It was a dramatic debut. Gonzalez stopped to help Hawthorn and the car slipped backwards and collided with the English driver's 625. There was a

terrible fire. Hawthorn, the "Farnham flyer" spent several days in hospital.

1954 was a difficult year. Ferrari was powerless against Fangio who swept on to his third world title, first with Maserati and then with Mercedes. Then Ascari and Villoresi left Maranello. In Turin, the new Formula 1 Lancia was taking shape under the guidance of Vittorio Jano. Ferrari scored only two victories: at Silverstone with Froilan Gonzalez in the 625 (yes, him again, a repeat of the battle with Alfa Romeo of the 14th of July 1951) and in Spain—the last

Grand Prix of the season—with Mike Hawthorn in the 553. But the "silver arrows", in their twin versions—with and without fairings over the wheels—dominated the field.

In 1955, the 553 became the 555. The "Shark" became the "Supershark". The rear suspension was completely contained within the frame. Another reserve tank was mounted behind the driver in addition to the two lateral tanks.

This new 555 carried many hopes with it. But yet again it was to be the 625 which produced the only Ferrari win of the season when Maurice Trintignant drove it to victory at the Monaco Grand Prix. In reality, this car had a 625 chassis but the engine roaring under the bonnet was a 555.

The "Supershark" made its debut at the Bordeaux circuit, with Nino Farina and Maurice Trintignant, neither of whom finished.

It made its first appearance in a world championship event at Monaco with Piero Taruffi and Harry Schell. Paul Frére took over from Taruffi and came in eighth while Schell withdrew.

The 555 picked up good placings in Belgium, Holland and in Italy at Monza. The Supershark's last world title race was the 1956 Argentine Grand Prix. This was the end of Aurelio Lampredi's four cylinder engine and he left Ferrari.

In the meantime, Lancia had withdrawn from competition and had bequeathed its racing equipment and personnel to Ferrari. For the entire 1956 season, Ferrari used the eight cylinder D 50s. The Mercedes had left the stage. And Fangio won his fourth world title with Maranello. Ferrari now had three titles under his belt. The D 50s became Ferrari 801s in 1957. Fangio, who had left Maranello for Maserati, won his fifth world title, a record which remains unbeaten.

The car illustrated in these pages was used by Maurice Trintignant at the end of 1955. It has been restored and fitted with a new engine.

Engine: 4 in line. Displacement: 2497,6 cc. Bore and stroke: 100x79,5 mm. Compression ratio: 14:1. Power: 260 bhp at 7400 rpm. Valve gear: 2 valves per cylinder, dohc. Fuel system: atmospheric induction, two horizontal twin carburettors. Ignition: twin plug, 2 magnetos. Gearbox: 5 speeds + reverse in unit with the differential. Brakes: drum. Frame: tubular steel ladder. Suspension, front: unequal A-arms, double wishbones, coil springs, antiroll bar. Suspension, rear: de Dion axle, 2 trailing arms, transverse leaf spring, lever-action shock absorbers. Tracks: 1278 mm (front), 1250 mm (rear). Wheelbase: 2160 mm. Weight: 600 kg (dry).

DINO 156 F2

The last front engined F2 single seater. The engine was that 65° V6 which Ferrari's son Dino had wanted so much before his tragically early death in 1956. A long career: from 1957 to 1960. It debuted in the Naples Grand Prix with Luigi Musso, April 29th1957. The first win at Reims came that same year, with Maurice Trintignant.

While the 8-cylinder Ferrari '801' was defeated by Maserati in the 1957 world championship, a 65° V6 engine was taking shape. It was the brainchild of Ferrari's young son, Dino. Aurelio Lampredi had a hand in its development before he left Ferrari, as did Vittorio Jano. In that period it was in the hands of Bellentani and Fraschetti. The latter was to be involved in a fatal accident while testing a modified F2 at the Modena autodrome. The 156 F2 represented the first step towards the realization of the 246 F1. It was ready in 1956, the year of Dino's death from a rare form of muscular dystrophy. In a moving memorial letter, Ferrari wrote:

"Among the many things which remind me of you there is the angry wail of the new born engine—do you remember that little engine whose cause you pleaded during the long snowy evenings of last winter?—it was a 'pup' whose cry you never heard; but it will bear your name and so all will remember your infinite passion."

The 156 F2 was powered by a 65° V6 engine. The angle was chosen in order to achieve a better fit for the double overhead camshafts and the inlet passages. Displacement: 1489.35 cc. Bore: 70 mm. Stroke: 64.5 mm. Power, at the end of 1957: 180 bhp at 9.000 rpm. The body was similar to that of the 801 F1 with the exception that the bonnet air

intake fairing had been extended to the cockpit.

The 29th April 1957 saw its debut at the Naples Grand Prix. Cars from the senior Formula also took part in the race. The 156 was not a disappointment, and showed agility and manoeuverability. Luigi Musso took third place. Then the car was used during practice for the Monaco Grand Prix, but it did not race. The first win came in a Formula 2 event at Reims on the 4th of July. Maurice Trintignant managed to beat the rear engined Cooper. In 1958, at Reims again, it came second behind Behra's Porsche. By that time the front was the same as the 246 F1 (still with the exception of the air intake on the bonnet). In 1959, at the Siracusa GP, Behra had to struggle against the Coopers with the Coventry Climax or Borgward engines. The Cooper driven by Stirling Moss had the latter engine and it won the race. But Behra took second place in the 156. The car was also entered for the Monaco GP, with Cliff Allison. The Englishman was involved in an accident caused by von

Trips' Porsche and he did not finish. In the Formula 2 event at Reims, run concomitant with the French Grand Prix, Allison was obliged to withdraw again. Behra was fifth in the Zandvoort Grand Prix. The 156 raced during the following season as well. With von Trips at the wheel, it won the Siracusa Grand Prix. The car was by that time a real F1 "prototype". 4 overhead camshafts. 180 bhp. Disc brakes all round. Independent rear suspension. The evolution of the engine was interesting. It started with 1500 cc, then 1860 cc, then 2195 cc, and finally 2417.33 cc. The 1860 cc version debuted at the Modena Grand Prix of the 22nd September 1957. Musso was second, Collins fourth. The 2200 and the 2400 engines, for Howthorn and Collins respectively, were mounted on the cars for the first time for a luckless attempt at the Moroccan GP on the 22nd October 1957. These pages show the 1959 version of the 156 F2.

With this car Jean Behra took part in the 1959 Siracusa Grand Prix (2nd) and the Zandvoort Grand Prix (5th). In 1960 Wolfgang von Trips won the Siracusa Grand Prix in it and the American driver Richie Ginther took second place in the Modena Grand Prix that same year.

Engine: front 65° V-6. Displacement: 1489,35 cc. Bore and stroke: 70x64,5 mm. Compression ratio: 10:1. Power: 180 bhp at 9000 rpm. Valve gear: 2 valves per cylinder, dohc. Fuel system: atmospheric induction, three carburettors. Ignition: 2 magnetos. Gearbox: transverse rear, 4 speeds + reverse. Brakes: hydraulic drum. Frame: tubular. Suspension, front: independent, unequal length A-arms, coil springs. Suspension, rear: de Dion axle, transverse leaf spring. Tracks: 1270 mm (front), 1250 mm (rear). Wheelbase: 2160 mm. Weight: 512 kg (dry)

246 F1

The last front engined F1 Ferrari. The last of its type to win a Grand Prix: Phil Hill's victory at Monza in 1960. It is the car in which Mike Hawthorn won the '58 world title. The 6 cylinder Dino was finally right on target.

The 801s could not get the better of Juan Manuel Fangio in the Maserati who went on to win his fifth world title in 1957. Ferrari sought revenge with his usual tenacity introducing the 246 F1 in 1958. This was a 2500 cc 6-cylinder single-seater which remained in the line-up until 1960, the year of the demise of the 2.5 litre formula.

It was developed on the Dino 156 F2 chassis. The engine was derived from the 1500 cc Dino engine, so called in memory of Ferrari's son Alfredo who died tragically young. An experimental car had already appeared in 1957 at the Modena Grand Prix, where it had taken a promising second place. At first, the engine was 1860 cc, but by the Morocco Grand Prix at the end of the year the displacement had already been upgraded to 2417.3 cc.

The 246 used two engines in the 1958-60 period: the 2417 cc version in '58 and the 2474 cc type 256 version in the following seasons.

The 246 won the world championship in 1958. But Cooper and Vanwall made life difficult. Mike Hawthorn took

the title with only one outright victory, the French Grand Prix, to his credit. At that time it was worth a point to record the fastest lap and the "Farnham Flyer" picked up a good five of them. Moss, his closest rival, won three more races but took fewer placings and fastest lap times. Happy times for Ferrari, certainly, but things were often dramatic too: Luigi Musso died at Reims and Peter Collins was killed at the Nürburgring. Perhaps moved by these events, Mike Hawthorn, the first Englishman to take the world title, decided to quit racing. But a cruel destiny decreed that he too was to die in a road accident on a January day in 1959. From a technical standpoint, the season had shown that the V6 was reliable. Its power had grown in the course of the year: from 275 bhp at 8300 rpm to 285 at 8500 rpm. Plus the novelties: first, self-ventilated drum brakes; then disc brakes. Then the tubular chassis with small diameter tubing.

Now Ferrari had to fight it out with the English instead of the Germans. The rear-engined Cooper-Climaxes swept the board and gave Jack Brabham the world title in 1959 and 1960. A lot of things had changed at Ferrari for the 1959 season. von Trips had left and Tony Brooks, Cliff Allison, Jean Behra and Dan Gurney were hired.

The 246 was modified. All the cars were fitted with disc brakes, Dunlop tyres and the five speed gearbox. Coil springs and Koni telescopic shock absorbers replaced the leaf springs and the Houdaille dampers. At the end of the year, at the US Grand Prix at

Sebring, Brooks' car was fitted for the first time with fully independent rear suspension with unequal A-arms and coil springs. But all things considered 1959 was a disappointing year for Ferrari with only two wins, both of which were the work of Tony Brooks, in the French and German Grand Prix.

In 1960, the independent rear suspension was definitively adopted. Behra and Gurney left, but von Trips returned. Attempts were made to improve the trim of the 246 by refitting the lateral tanks (the lines resembled the "Shark" once more therefore). The engine was shifted slightly rearwards. Even though he was apparently reluctant to do so (had he not said that "the horses have to pull the cart, not push it"?), Ferrari espoused the idea of the rear engine. A car of this type made an appearance at Monte Carlo where Richie Ginther took it to sixth place. Then von Trips was given a real prototype (with a 1500 cc engine mounted at the rear) of the car which was to race in 1961—the 156 F1. Cooper, BRM and Lotus did not take part at Monza as they considered the famous high speed oval too dangerous. Their absence had no influence on the outcome of the championship because Jack

Brabham was already world champion. This race at Monza was the swan song of the 246 which Phil Hill drove to an unexpected victory. It was his first Grand Prix win, and the only one for Ferrari that season. And the last one for a front-engined Ferrari. In fifth place (but first among the Formula 2 entries) was von Trips in the rear-engined 1500 cc; a fact which augured well for 1961. The 246 FI shown in these pages is the car in which Phil Hill won at Monza. Subsequently, Ferrari replaced the Dino engine with a 3 litre V12 Testarossa and sent the single-seater off to New Zealand. Pat Hoare drove it in the Tasman Cup. The present owner bought the car with the V12 engine in 1978.

Engine: front 65° V-6. Displacement: 2147,3 cc. Bore and stroke: 85x71 mm (1958). Compression ratio: 9,8:1. Power: 280 bhp at 8500 rpm. Valve gear: 2 valves per cylinder, sohc. Fuel system: atmospheric induction, three twin-barrel, downdraft carburettors. Ignition: twin plug, 2 distributors and 4 coils. Gearbox: 4 speeds + reverse, rear in unit with the differential. Brakes: self ventilated drum. Frame: tubular steel ladder. Suspension, front: unequal A-arms, double wishbones, coil springs, telescopic shock absorbers, antiroll bar. Suspension, rear: de Dion axle, upper transverse leaf spring, 2 trailing arms, Houdaille dampers. Tracks: 1270 mm (front), 1240 mm (rear). Wheelbase: 2160 mm. Weight: 560 kg (dry).

512 F1

Debuted in practice For the 1964 Italian Grand Prix with Lorenzo Bandini. The engine was a flat twelve by Mauro Forghieri. First race: the US Grand Prix at Watkins Glen. It was used until the end of 1965, but it never won.

In 1961, the first year of the new 1500 cc formula, Ferrari scored a bullseye to win its fifth world championship with the American driver Phil Hill. The car was the "156 F1" designed by Carlo Chiti. The engine was a classic 6 cylinder Dino but the V went through a variety of angulations: 60, 65 and 120. This car was used until 1964. The famous air intakes over the front radiators reminded people of a shark's nose. Practically invincible in 1961 (it won 7 out of 9 Grand Prix), it did not achieve good results in the following seasons. Graham Hill won the '62 title in the BRM and Jim Clark won the '63 version with the Lotus.

Carlo Chiti, along with some other executives, left Ferrari and the end of '61 thus paving the way for a reshuffle of the technical staff at Maranello. This was to bear fruit rather later on, in 1964. '64 was the year in which Ferrari won its sixth world title with John Surtees and the 90° V8 engine. A difficult period began for Ferrari at the outset of 1965. The 158 could not keep up with the Lotus and BRM, and the 512 fitted with the flat 12 engine was not emerging as a

contender. The 90° V8 which powered the 158 had been developed by Angelo Bellei with Vittorio Jano as consultant. Mauro Forghieri was responsible for the flat twelve in the 512.

These two engines, and the cars which were to be powered by them, had a parallel but slightly disjointed history, in the sense that Bellei's 8-cylinder engine was the first to be raced while the history of the 12 was rather less straightforward. Apart from the engines, the 158 and 512 were identical. With the exception of one small difference: the 512 has a wheelbase which is barely 2 mm longer than that of its sister car. Otherwise the only way to tell the difference is to look at the number of the intake trumpets. Both cars have an aluminum monocoque with the

engine, gearbox and differential forming an integral part of the frame like the Lotus 25. John Surtees took the world championship with the 158

while Ferrari looked to the future on the basis of Forghieri's 12-cylinder unit. The 512 made its first appearance at the Italian Grand Prix at Monza

Engine: rear flat 12. Displacement: 1489,6 cc. Bore and stroke: 56x50,4 mm. Compression ratio: 9,8:1. Power: 225 bhp at 11500 rpm. Valve gear: 2 valves per cylinder. Fuel system: Bosch injection. Ignition: single plug, 2 distributors and 2 coils. Gearbox: 5 speeds + reverse, cantilevered, longitudinal. Brakes: discs (rear inboard). Suspension, front: unequal A-arms, upper rocking arm, lower wishbone, coil springs, inboard coaxial dampers. Suspension, rear: unequal A-arms, coaxial spring-dampers, 2 trailing arms. Tracks: 1350 mm (front), 1340 mm (rear). Wheelbase: 2400 mm. Weight: 475 kg.

where Lorenzo Bandini put the car through its paces during the Saturday practice session. The car was not used for the race. Its real debut was to be at the US Grand Prix at Watkins Glen, still with Bandini at the wheel. It bore the white and blue livery of Luigi Chinetti's North American Racing Team because Ferrari had sent back his competitor's license in protest against the fact that the 250 LM had not received its GT homologation. Bandini was obliged to withdraw. In the Mexican Grand Prix, the next race and the last appointment of that season, Bandini scored a good third place. Owing to the way the race was run (with Bandini at Surtees' service), it could be said that the 158 won the world title thanks to the help of the 512. Since the new formula was planned for 1966, the 512 had only one year of life ahead of it. Not enough time for it to give of its best. However, despite this brief lifetime, the 512 engine underwent some important changes.

The Lucas fuel injection system was scrapped in favour of Bosch injection. Twin plug ignition was adopted. The camshafts, injectors and cylinder heads were modified. In its final version, the engine delivered 225 bhp at 11.500 rpm. The career of the 512 F1 came to a close at the end of 1965. It never won. The best result was Lorenzo Bandini's second place at Mante Carlo. The end of the season saw Jim Clark's victory in the Lotus 33. The 512 F1 shown in these pages is the one which debuted at Watkins Glen in 1964. The next year, Bandini raced it in South Africa, at Siracusa, in the Silverstone International Trophy, in Monaco, Belgium and France.

John Surtees drove it in England and Holland and Pedro Rodriguez took his place for one of the last world championship events: Watkins Glen.

DINO 166 F2

The Dino continued to show its versatility. It showed up again in 1967 in the 166 F2. A Rouen debut, with Jonathan Williams. The entire 1968 season spent chasing a win. It came in October, at Hockenheim, thanks to an Italian driver, Tino Brambilla. It won the Temporada Argentina with Andrea De Adamich.
The Dino V6 engine was already twelve years old but it was still efficient. Its development included displacements ranging from 1500 cc to 2500 cc. Both the 2417 cc and the 1500 cc version defended Ferrari's Formula 1 colours. It was fitted to sports cars (the 166 Dino with the 1600 cc engine), it won the Europeo della Montagna (Scarfiotti, Dino 166) in 1962 and 1965 (Scarfiotti, Dino 206). In 1968, thanks to an agreement with Fiat, who were interested in a high performance GT, Ferrari was able to take part in the Formula 2 championship

reserved for cars produced in numbers of at least 500.
The Dino 166 F2 was introduced for the first time at the Turin sports car show of 1967.
This version had a 1596.2 cc engine with a low stroke to bore ratio (45.8 to 86), a Heron type head with three valves per cylinder and twin camshafts. The gearbox was identical to that of the Dino prototype. A characteristic of the body was the extremely short wheelbase (2200 mm) with the elevated cross section.
The Dino F2 made its debut at Rouen on the 9th of July 1967. The car was not the same any more. The head now had three

valves, no longer side by side but set at an angle to one another, rather like the lay out in the Dino prototype, and with twin plug ignition. The gearbox was a new twin shaft type which was later used in F1 cars too. Jonathan Williams, who was driving that day, failed to finish.
The V-6 engine underwent further development. A new four valve head was adopted. On February 21st 1968, Ferrari tested the new version of the 166 F2 at Vallelunga and Modena. In its definitive form, the 166 F2 had the 1593.4 cc engine with bore and stoke of 79.5x53.3. Maximum power was 225 bhp at 11.000 rpm.
The first appearance in the F2 European Trophy was made at the Barcellona Grand Prix on the 31st of March. Amon was third and Ickx did not finish. Then came Hockenheim, Nürburgring, Zolder. Ickx's partial success in

the second heat run over the Belgian circuit seemed to be a hopeful sign. But victory was slow in arriving: Crystal Palace, Coppa del Reno, Gran Premio Lotteria di Monza, Tulln Langenlebarn, Zandvoort, Pergusa, none of these races was to produce the hoped for result. A full blooded victory finally came when Tino Brambilla took the Baden Württemberg Grand Prix at Hockenheim on the 13th of October. A sensational double followed at the Rome Grand Prix with Brambilla first and De Adamich second. The latter was just back after the accident which had cost him months of enforced inactivity. The Dino 166 F2 continued this good run of results with a win in the Temporada Argentina. Brambilla had one win and De Adamich won twice

to take the trophy. Ferrari neglected the 1969 Formula 2 championship. No significant results were achieved in the first races of the season. The Dino's last appearance as a works car dates from the Gran Premio Lotteria di Monza of the 22nd June. Then Ferrari withdrew them. But the following year, at Monza again, Tino Brambilla gave a privately entered Dino 166 F2 its last important result: a third place.
The Dino 166 F2 shown in these

pages took part in the following races in 1968: Siracusa (Derek Bell 5th), Rome (De Adamich 2nd), and the Temporada Argentina, in which De Adamich came second in Buenos Aires, first in Cordoba, San Juan and Buenos Aires again. In 1969, Derek Bell failed to finish in this car at Thruxton, came fifth at the Nürburgring and at Monza, and eighth at Jarama. Clay Regazzoni was disqualified at the start of the Deutschland Trophy at Hockenheim .

Engine: rear 65° V-6. Displacement: 1593,4 cc. Bore and stroke: 79,5x53,3 mm. Compression ratio: 11,2:1. Power: 225 bhp at 11.000 rpm. Valve gear: 4 overhead camshafts, 4 valves per cylinder. Fuel system: Lucas indirect injection. Ignition: distributors, 1 spark plug per cylinder. Gearbox: 5 speeds + reverse. Brakes: discs. Suspension, front: unequal length A-arms. Suspension, rear: Unequal length A-arms and radius arms (rear). Tracks: 1405 mm (front), 1435 mm (rear). Wheelbase: 2250 mm. Weight: 420 kg (dry).

DINO 246
TASMANIA

The version with the 2400 cc 166 F2 Dino engine. Prepared for the 1968 Tasmania Cup. Driven by the New Zealander, Chris Amon, it was beaten to the line by a fraction. The following year, the English driver, Derek Bell, drove the model presented here in the same race. He took fourth place.
Ferrari took part in the 1968 Tasmanian championship with one car which was in the hands of Chris Amon. The car, officially known as the Dino

246 Tasmania, was both old and new at the same time. The engine derived from the first of the Dino units, the 2500 cc (approx.) 60° V6 engine which had been mounted on the last Ferrari single-seaters made for the two and a half litre formula, valid until 1960. Since then, the structure had been profoundly developed. The V formed by the two banks of cylinders had increased to 65 degree. The fuel system was Lucas fuel injection (but there was also a Dino 1500 cc with

Bosch injection). There were three valves per cylinder, two inlet and one exhaust. The ignition had two spark plugs per cylinder. In the various stages of development this engine was also used in the 2400 cc 6 cylinder single-seater: it served as an experimental vehicle when the three litre Formula 1 was just beginning. It was driven by Bandini in the first races of the 1966 championship.
The components of the frame and the transmission were

completely new. The gearbox was the recent twin shaft type used in the F1 and F2 single-seaters. The body was the same as that of the 1600 cc F2, from which it differed most of all in the wheel size. The power was 285 bhp at 8900 rpm. In 1968 the Tasman championship consisted of eight events; 4 races in New Zealand, three in Australia and one in Tasmania. These took place in the period between the 6th of January and the 4th of March. Jim Clark had won the championship of the previous year in the 2000 cc Lotus-Climax V8. The Scottish

ace had been up against the other Scot, Jackie Stewart, in his BRM V8 2000 and Jack Brabham in his Brabham-Repco V8 2500. Ferrari had not taken part in the championship. The Ferrari expedition was led by Gianni Marelli, 27, and Roger Bailey, who had taken leave from Alan Mann Racing. They decided to use both the 4 valve per cylinder engine, which was more powerful yet more delicate (and in fact at Surfer's Paradise it was to overheat) and the three valve. Chris Amon won the first event at Pukekohe after a furious

struggle with Jim Clark and his Lotus-Ford 2500 cc. Clark failed to finish. This was the New Zealander's first victory in a single-seater. In the second race, at Levin, Amon did it again while Clark dropped out a second time. Amon had made his debut ten years before on this very track in an Austin A 40. In the third race, at Christchurch, Jim Clark finally won and Amon took second place. Bruce McLaren won at Invercargill and Amon was fourth after being held up by an about-face due to an oil leak which finished up all over the rear wheels of his car. The New Zealander dropped out with a burned out head gasket at Brisbane. Clark won there and the race for the Cup had become a ding dong affair between the two. Clark won again at Warwick Farm where Amon was only fourth and the Scot went to the top of the

table. Amon was beaten again when Clark romped to a runaway victory at Melbourne. Then Piers Courage won the last event at Longford in a McLaren-Ford, with Clark fourth. The Scot had won the title again. Towards the end of the year Derek Bell tested the '69 version of the Dino 246 Tasmania at the Modena autodrome. It was derived from the car which had taken part in that year's European Formula 2 championship with Jack Ickx (dropped out in Barcellona and the Nurburgring, fourth at Zolder in the final points table, fifteenth at Crystal Palace, sixth at Pergusa), and with Derek Bell (did not finish at Monza, seventh at Tulln-Langenlebarn in the final points table, fourteenth in the Zandvoort final, third at Hockenheim, sixth at Vallelunga in the final points table). Many people thought that Tino Brambilla had won at

Hockenheim with this car but, according to Doug Nye's precise testimony, the frame of the 166 F2 used by the Italian driver on that occasion did not

bear the number 0010 but 0004.

In the 1969 Tasman Cup, the Dino 246 shown in these pages took fourth place in the final rankings with Derek Bell at the wheel. In the first Cup event at Pukekohe, the English driver came fourth. Then he did not finish at Levin, came fifth in Christchurch and Teretonga, second at Lakeside and Warwick Farm, and finally fifth at Sandown Park.

Before racing in Tasmania,

Derek Bell had some experience with Ferraris in the European Formula 2 championship as well as in some Formula 1 events in 1968. He debuted in a 166 F2 on the 23rd of June 1968 at the Gran Premio Lotteria di Monza. Very fast in practice, he was unlucky in the race: who could forget that terrible pile-up which was to

upset the progress of the event? It was thanks to Ferrari that the Englishman got his first Formula 1 drives: first at Oulton Park, in a non-title race, and then in the Italian and the US Grand Prix. He withdrew on all three occasions. When he came back from the Tasman Cup he drove a Ferrari in a Formula 1 event (Silverstone, 9th) and in four Formula 2 events.

Then he left Maranello.

Engine: rear 65° V-6. Displacement: 2405 cc. Bore and stroke: 90x63 mm. Compression ratio: 11,5:1. Power: 285 bhp at 8900 rpm. Valve gear: two overhead camshafts per bank of cylinders, 3 valves per cylinder. Fuel system: Lucas injection. Ignition: distributors, 2 spark plugs per cylinder. Gearbox: 5 speeds + reverse. Brakes: discs. Suspension, front: fully independent, unequal length A-arms. Suspension, rear: unequal length A-arms and radius arms. Tracks: 1405 mm (front), 1400 mm (rear). Wheelbase: 2220 mm. Weight: 425 kg.

DINO 246
TASMANIA

Chris Amon won the 1969 Tasman Cup in this car. He beat drivers of the calibre of Jochen Rindt, Graham Hill, Piers Courage and Jack Brabham. Four wins out of seven races. The next year, in the same car, Graeme Lawrence won the same Cup.

Having nearly won in 1968, Chris Amon hit the target in the 1969 Tasmanian Cup. These pages show the car which the New Zealander drove to victory.

The 0008 chassis had also been used in the 1968 European Formula 2 Trophy. Amon took it to third place on its debut at the Barcellona Grand Prix. Then it came eighth in the Rhine Cup and twelfth in the final points table at the Tulln Langenlebarn event in Vienna. The same car had been driven by Brian Redman (fourth in the Eifel Grand Prix at the Nürburgring) and Tino Brambilla (third in the Mediterranean Grand Prix at Pergusa).

However it was the Tasmania '69 version with the 2405 cc engine

which was to achieve the first successes.

This series of races in New Zealand and Australia had been established with the aim of keeping old cars in racing, preferably with local drivers at the wheel. But the abundant prizes had attracted the stars of the European circuit. In 1969, there was Jochen Rindt, who had just joined Lotus and who was eager to make his mark, and Graham Hill, also with Lotus and just as keen not to let his young teammate and rival beat him. Then there was Piers Courage, who hoped to be able to take

advantage of the rivalry at the heart of the Lotus team. And Jack Brabham, who took part in the last race on the calendar. Ferrari did not send a works team. Maranello had decided to hand over the management of its Dinos to Amon who subsequently raced in the colours of his own stable and paid all the running expenses. Derek Bell was his partner.

"I really appreciated what Enzo Ferrari did for me, says Amon. He gave us all the spare parts we needed and backed that up with all the necessary technical information." Amon had the use of two completely overhauled 24 valve engines. His team was composed of Roger Bailey, Amon's long standing personal mechanic, Bruce Wilson, David Liddel and Peter Bell. Chris Amon won four of the seven races on the card. He was well ahead of Rindt and Courage in the classic final. On his home tracks, the New Zealander set a scorching pace, winning the first two events, at Pukekohe and Levin. In the third

Engine: rear 65° V-6. Displacement: 2405 cc. Bore and stroke: 90x63 mm. Compression ratio: 11,5:1. Power: 285 bhp at 8900 rpm. Valve gear: two overhead camshafts per bank of cylinders, 3 valves per cylinder. Fuel system: Lucas injection. Ignition: distributors, 2 spark plugs per cylinder. Gearbox: 5 speeds + reverse. Brakes: discs. Suspension, front: fully independent, unequal length A-arms. Suspension, rear: unequal length A-arms and radius arms. Tracks: 1405 mm (front), 1400 mm (rear). Wheelbase: 2220 mm. Weight: 425 kg.

and fourth races, at Christchurch and Teretonga, he had to be content with thirds. Rindt and Courage were the winners on those occasions. The Dinos seemed to be in difficulty: the trim was not suited to those circuits and above all the rear spoiler was too small. But despite these problems Amon won again at Lakeside. This victory meant he was already the Tasman champion. In the penultimate race, at Warwick Farm, he got into trouble as Piers Courage went into a slide just after the start and had to withdraw. He finished in grand style though, as he took the Sandown Park event, the last one on the calendar. Along with Jochen Rindt, he recorded the fastest lap on three occasions,

more than any other driver in the seven races. Subsequently, Amon's car was sold to a local driver called Graeme Lawrence. In the 1970 championship Lawrence won at Levin on the 4th of January, and took a series of good placings. It was enough to beat the big Formula 5000s (on their first appearance in the Tasmania Cup) in the final rankings. With the same car, he took part in the South East Asia series, winning at Singapore and at Batu Tiga in Malaysia. In

the winter of '70-'71 he won the New Zealand Gold Star event. Then he tried to repeat the previous season's success in the Tasman Cup, but the Formula 5000s had taken over by then. The "little" Dino's days were numbered. Graeme Lawrence sold the car (which bore the number 14, his number in the Gold Star race) to the Frenchman Pierre Bardinon, the owner of the famous museum at Mas du Clos.
Today the car is in Italy.

59

312 B2

subsequently three, valves. While the 312 was evolving, a "246" was also racing with a 2400 cc 60° V6 engine which recalled that used for the formula in force between 1954 and 1960. Surtees' 312 won in Belgium, with the two valve variant, and Scarfiotti's three valve variant won in Italy. The Ferrari-Surtees split, which occurred during the season,

"B" as in boxer. 312 as in 3000 cc , 12-cylinder engine, debuted in practice for the 1971 South African Grand Prix. First win in the Brands Hatch Race of Champions with Clay Regazzoni. First world title race: Monaco '71. To its credit: 2 Grands Prix and a non-title race.

The new Formula came into force in 1966. It decreed a ceiling of 3000 cc for unsupercharged and 1500 cc for supercharged engines. Fuel was to be commercial blend and the minimum weight was 500 kilos. Ferrari took part in the world championship with the 312 (3 for 3000 cc, 12 for the number of cylinders), with an engine derived from the 275 P2, having an angulation of 60° and two,

affected team performance. The title went to Jack Brabham in the Brabham-Repco.

In 1967, the 312 was upgraded from 390 to 410 bhp, and weight was reduced thanks to the use of glass fibre for the bodywork. There were four valves per cylinder from Monza onwards. The car failed to win a world title event amid fierce competition. The

8-cylinder Ford-Cosworth engine entered the lists at the beginning of its long and gloriously successful career. Brabham-Repco won its second world championship, this time with Danny Hulme.

It was a dramatic season for Ferrari. Bandini was killed and Parkes injured. Scarfiotti hung up his helmet leaving Chris Amon to defend the Maranello colours along with Jonathan Williams, who raced in the last event of the season in Mexico.

The 312 was slimmed down even further in 1968 to reach the limit of 530 kilos. Two very young drivers lined up alongside Amon, the Belgian Jacky Ickx and the Italian Andrea De Adamich. The latter had a serious accident during the Race of Champions at Brands Hatch and was out of racing until the October. Ickx too was injured but he recovered in time to present Ferrari with its only win of the season when he took the French Grand Prix in the wet. The spoilers became a fixture from Belgium on and before the season was over the engine of the 312 was sporting a new head and modified camshafts. In 1969 the 312 was delivering 436 bhp at 11000 rpm. But Jacky Ickx was no longer driving it as he had left to join Brabham. Amon's bad luck continued and Ferrari did not win a Grand Prix. But development work on the boxer engine was continuing. In 1970, Ferrari lined up the new 312 B (B for boxer). A "flat" engine with 12 horizontally opposed cylinders. Displacement: 2991 cc. The crank shaft sat on only four bearing. Very compact, it delivered 450 bhp at 12000 rpm with only one spark plug per cylinder, 4 valves, chain driven double overhead camshafts. The frame had been completely reworked and parts of the body

were in glass fibre. Ickx returned and Regazzoni arrived. Ignazio Giunti also drove in two practice sessions. The first world title success for the 312 B, the Austrian Grand Prix, bore Jacky Ickx's signature. Then Regazzoni won at Monza; Ickx won again in Canada, and then in Mexico. But the world title went to the late Jochen Rindt.

The 312 B was in the line-up for the first part of the 1971 championship. Andretti won the South African Grand Prix and the Questor Grand Prix, a non-title event. Ickx took the Jochen Rindt Memorial trophy at Hockenheim. But from the Monaco Grand Prix onwards, the 312 B2 took the field. The B2 made its track debut during practice for the South African Grand Prix. Clay Regazzoni wrote it off and the debut had to be postponed. It had raced and won in the Race of Champions at Brands Hatch, still with Regazzoni, but this was a non-title event.

That success, plus Ickx's third place in Monaco and the world

championship debut of the 312 B2, caused hopes to rise. Ickx, who was a peerless driver in the wet, went on to take the Dutch Grand Prix. But the newborn hopes were soon dashed as the B2 began to suffer from serious lubrication and tyre problems. The season continued with a series of results which got worse and worse.

The B2 scored only one victory in

1972, but it was one of those which really count. Ickx won the German Grand Prix on the most technically demanding circuit in Formula 1: the Nürburgring. Regazzoni was second. Three pole positions, two fastest laps and second places in Spain and Monaco must also be taken into account. The car shown here is a unique 1972 312 B2 which is the property of a Swiss collector.

Engine: rear flat 12. Displacement: 2991,8 cc. Bore and stroke: 80x49,6 mm. Power: 470 bhp at 12.600 rpm. Valve gear: 4 valves per cylinder, dohc. Fuel system: Lucas injection. Ignition: single, capacitive ignition (Dinoplex) Magneti Marelli. Gearbox: 5 speeds + reverse overhanging longitudinal rear. Brakes: Lockheed discs and calipers (inboard rear). Frame: unitized monocoque, aluminium panels rivetted onto a tubular steel structure. Suspension, front: unequal A-arms, upper rocking arm, lower wishbone, inboard spring-dampers. Suspension, rear: single upper lateral link, lower wishbone, single upper trailing link, horizontal spring-dampers above the differential. Tracks: 1625 mm (front), 1605 mm (rear). Wheelbase: 2426 mm. Weight: 578 kg (dry). The data refer to the 1972 version.

312 B2

Another B2. There were some external differences with respect to the model shown in the preceding pages. It had the same engine but it had been renewed and upgraded. About 485 bhp. Driven by Regazzoni, Merzario, and Andretti.

A game of football was to make the 1972 season even more problematic than it ought to have been. Clay Regazzoni, an exuberant, cheerful type, broke his left wrist. Nanni Galli was asked to substitute for him in the French Grand Prix. It was neither a worthy nor a blameworthy debut for Galli, but his career with Ferrari was stalled nonetheless. Merzario drove the car in the English Grand Prix and he turned in an excellent performance taking sixth place in his first race in a single-seater. Mario Andretti could have become an important piece on Ferrari's game board, but he could only race when his many American commitments allowed him to. He took part in only five Grand Prix. The B2 was used in the first part of the 1973 season too. Clay Regazzoni had left Ferrari for BRM. In Argentina Ickx came fourth and Merzario ninth. But Merzario had the satisfaction of doing better than the Belgian in Brazil: they came fourth and fifth respectively. Merzario was fifth again in South Africa while Ickx did not finish. It was the B2's last race. The car's career performance is as follows: from the '71 Monaco Grand Prix to the '73 South African Grand Prix, it only managed three victories, of which one was in a non-title race. A rather disappointing balance for a car for which a glorious future had been predicted at its conception. Mauro Forghieri had worked on the aerodynamics as thoroughly as he had looked after the engine. Small fairings had appeared here and there in an attempt to create greater compactness. But the real problem with the B2 had to do with the horizontal springs of the rear suspension. In theory, they were supposed to ensure better roadholding, but this technical innovation made the

Engine: rear flat 12. Displacement: 2991,8 cc. Bore and stroke: 80x49,6 mm. Compression ratio: 11,5:1. Power: 470 bhp at 12.600 rpm. Valve gear: 4 valves per cylinder, dohc. Fuel system: Lucas injection. Ignition: electronic (Dinoplex). Gearbox: 5 speeds + reverse, cantilevered longitudinal rear. Brakes: discs (inboard rear). Frame: monocoque, aluminium panels rivetted onto a tubular steel structure. Suspension, front: unequal A-arms, upper rocking arm, lower wishbone, inboard spring-dampers. Suspension, rear: twin wishbones, single upper lateral link, horizontal spring above the differential. Tracks: 1625 mm (front), 1605 mm (rear). Wheelbase: 2426 mm. Weight: 578 kg. The data refer to the 1972 version.

car hard to drive in practice and the drivers complained of annoying vibration. It was found necessary therefore to alter the classic geometry of the suspension. Insufficient lubrication was another problem which emerged in 1971 and Forghieri struggled to find a solution. Various engine types were tried. From a version supplying 470 bhp at 12600 rpm with a compression ratio of 11.5:1, they moved on to a 485 bhp unit with a bore and stroke of 80 mm x 49.6 mm. The power to weight ratio was one of the best around at that time: 1.11 kilos per horsepower.

The new B3 first appeared on the track at Fiorano in the August of '72. Both Ickx and Regazzoni tested it. The former driver ran over a

hare in it and *utosprint* nicknamed the car the Formula 1 "Safari". The comment continued: "It looks like a bulldozer, or a motor mower. One thing is certain: that with a short wheelbase like that, it's easy to drive. As you know, the B3 derives from Rocchi's Indy '71 project which was realized with the help of Forghieri, the sidelined technical director at Ferrari. It seems that he had difficulties with the new technical staff, Colombo and Giorgio Ferrari, regarding the preparation of the new B3." The B2 shown in these pages is owned by an Italian collector. Clay Regazzoni drove it in Spain on the 1st May 1972,

and took third place. Arturo Merzario drove it at the German Grand Prix at the Nürburgring on the 30th of July, but he could do no better than eleventh. Mario Andretti took it to the Italian G.P. at Monza, but he had to be content with seventh place. The car was Merzario's in 1973. It took part in two races: Argentina and Brazil. He came eighth in the first race, while his teammate Jacky Ickx was fourth in another B2. Merzario did better in the second race by coming fourth to Ickx's fifth. The exterior of the car was not exactly the same as the model shown in the preceding pages but it had a renovated and upgraded version of the same engine.

312 B3

Debut in the 1973 Spanish Grand Prix, with Jacky Ickx. A disappointing season. But the next year, in its fourth version, the B3 racked up three victories, ten pole positions and many placings. It ran its last Grand Prix races in Argentina and Brazil in 1975.

The B3 which had been seen at Fiorano in the August of 1972 was the so-called "snowplough". The car had been Mauro Forghieri's particular responsibility, as well as a source of friction between himself and his two colleagues who, along with himself, formed a triumvirate at the head of the Maranello technical staff in those days. It was low and flat with a large frontal area. It weighed 540 kilos. This first version of the B3 did not last long as Ferrari decided to cut short its development. A second version, this time under the supervision of Sandro Colombo, was ready by the February of 1973. The monocoque was made in England. It was one of the rare occasions in which Ferrari had such a job done abroad. The engine was integral with the chassis. It developed 485 bhp at 12500 rpm with a compression ratio of 11.5:1. Novelties included lateral radiators mounted ahead of the rear wheels, and a deformable structure in line with the new regulations.

The B3 debuted in the Spanish GP with Jacky Ickx who could

only manage a disappointing 12th place. Things did not get better in the ensuing races. The Belgian did not finish at Zolder and Monaco, was sixth in Sweden, fifth in France, and eighth in England. Arturo Merzario failed to finish in Monaco and came seventh in France. The anxiety which was gnawing at the heart of the team became critical around the time of the German Grand Prix. Ferrari, dissatisfied with the B3's results up to that point, had decided not to race in Holland and Germany. Ickx raced in a McLaren at the Nürburgring. The "technical troika—

Forghieri, Colombo and Ferrari—was put on ice and Forghieri returned with full powers. In short order he produced a new version of the B3. This car, indicated by the cypher "S" ("sperimentale") had the air intake above the roll bar in a unit with the front spoiler. The two water radiators were set obliquely ahead of the rear suspension. The oil radiator was mounted, still longitudinally, on the left side body. The geometry of the suspension was completely rethought. This third version of the B3 made its debut in Austria where Arturo Merzario started in the third row. He had a fine race and was running a solid fourth until a drop in engine performance caused him to slip back to seventh place. Merzario withdrew at Monza and Ickx was only eighth in what was his last race with Ferrari. Merzario was left alone to take on the American adventure: he was fifteenth in Canada; sixteenth in the States.

The fourth version of the B3 was made ready for the 1974 season. The engine was slightly more powerful: 495 bhp at 12600 rpm. The driving position was further forward and the air intake behind the driver was much higher. Various types of stabilizers appeared. Luca Cordero di Montezemolo replaced Peter Schetty as racing manager and Regazzoni returned. Above all, Niki Lauda joined the team. Mauro

Forghieri retained full technical responsibility for the development of the car. Things began to work. After the good placings in Argentina and Brazil and the withdrawals in South Africa, Ferrari found its winning ways once more at the Spanish Grand Prix. It was a double at that: Niki Lauda first, Clay Regazzoni second.

Ferrari had not won a Grand Prix since the 30th of July 1972 (when Jacky Ickx won at the Nürburgring with the B2). The B3 continued to win: Lauda in Holland, Regazzoni in Germany. The Swiss was in with a chance of the title. The struggle with Emerson Fittipaldi was decided in the last race of the season, the US Grand Prix. Regazzoni, afflicted by technical problems, could do no better than 11th place and Fittipaldi was the champion. But Ferrari was back at the top of Formula 1 with a bang. The season had been a positive one: three wins, 10 pole positions out of 15 races, lots of good placings.

The B3 raced in the first two Grand Prix of 1975. Argentina: Regazzoni fourth, Lauda fifth. Brazil: Regazzoni fourth again, Lauda sixth.

But in the meanwhile the 312T was taking its first steps. The version of the B3 shown here is the one driven by Jacky Ickx in 1973: Spain (10th), Belgium (DNF), Monaco (DNF), Sweden (6th), France (5th), England (8th), Italy (8th). Lauda also drove it in the 1974 Monaco Grand Prix (DNF). The position of the radiators is worthy of note: they have been shifted to the sides of the car.

Engine: rear flat 12. Displacement: 2991,8 cc. Bore and stroke: 80x49,6 mm. Compression ratio: 11,5:1. Power: 485 bhp at 12.500 rpm. Valve gear: 4 valves per cylinder, dohc. Fuel system: Lucas injection. Ignition: single plug, capacitive ignition (Dinoplex) Magneti Marelli. Gearbox: 5 speeds + reverse, overhanging longitudinal rear. Brakes: Lockheed discs and calipers (inboard rear). Frame: unitized monocoque in boxed sheet aluminium. Suspension, front: twin wishbones, inboard spring-dampers. Suspension, rear: single upper lateral link, reversed lower wishbone, single upper trailing link, single lower leading link. Tracks: 1625 mm (front), 1605 mm (rear). Wheelbase: 2500 mm. Weight: 578 kg (dry). The data refer to the 1973 version.

312 T

"T" as in traverse: the position of the gearbox-differential unit. This is the car which took Ferrari back to the top of Formula 1 after an eleven year famine. Niki Lauda won his first, and Ferrari's seventh title.

An 11 year fast. It had lasted since Surtees' world championship win in the 158 back in 1964. Ferrari's seventh championship victory finally arrived in 1975 with Niki Lauda, in his second season with Ferrari, and the 312 T.

T stands for the transversely mounted gear-box-differential assembly.

The 312 T was the first Maranello built car to make its mark on the Formula which had

been in force since 1966. A completely new single-seater which only had one "old" thing about it—the engine—the 12-cylinder "boxer" which had been used for the first time on the 312 B2 in 1970. But this engine had redesigned heads, produced more torque at low revs, and was able to pump out 500 bhp at 12200 rpm. The frame was new as was the suspension, and the narrow, tapered nose supported the built-in air intake. This had been the fruit of long study in the wind tunnel aimed at improving the flow of air.

Mauro Forghieri remarked: "Work on the 312 T was developed in '74 when the revised B3 was still racing. In

fact the B3 already possessed many of the features of the T. It was a car which first saw the light as a design idea in '72. The first tests were made in '73 and advantage was taken of the work done on the B3. You could say that the B3 was the racing laboratory for the development of the T. We tried to exploit the space more rationally, with an eye to greater compactness. The aerodynamics were our particular concern, above all internally. This is to say that we tried, even more than we did with the B3, to use the `dirty' areas for cooling purposes while leaving the good parts unaltered. The T was a lot newer than its external appearance suggested."

It was introduced in the October of 1974. Much testing followed before the debut at the South African GP on the 10th March 1975. Lauda was fifth, Regazzoni sixteenth (practically speaking he had withdrawn with a broken throttle cable). Niki Lauda scored the first win with the "312 T" in a non-title race: the International Trophy at Silverstone. The first championship success came at Monaco, still with Niki Lauda. Ferrari had not won in the twisting city streets since Maurice Trintignant had pulled it off in the "625" in 1955. In the previous Grand Prix, raced over Montjuich in Spain, Lauda and Regazzoni had knocked each other out of contention after both had started in the front row. But it was not their fault. Andretti had rammed Lauda, who crashed into Regazzoni as a result. After Monaco, Lauda won in Belgium and Sweden. Three straight wins and the Austrian had staked a serious claim to the championship. His teammate Regazzoni was less brilliant: he withdrew at Monaco, came fifth in Belgium, third in Sweden. Lauda won again, in France and

the USA. Then, in the Italian Grand Prix at Monza, Regazzoni won the race and Lauda had to be content with the world championship.
The T continued winning the following season. Lauda won the first two Grand Prix in Argentina and Brazil. Regazzoni won at Long Beach. A car was given to the Everest stable and Giancarlo Martini raced it in two non-title events. In the Race of Champions

at Brands Hatch Martini was involved in an accident during the reconnaissance lap. A month later, in the International Trophy at Silverstone, he came tenth. This was the T's last appearance. Out of the fifteen Grand Prix for which it was entered it won eight times, took ten pole positions, and made eight fastest laps. It also won two non-title events: Lauda at Silverstone, Regazzoni at Dijon. Ferrari had not won so much since the days of the 500, when Alberto Ascari won the world title twice in a row in '52 and '53.
The 312 T shown in these pages is the one which Lauda drove to fifth place in the South African GP of 1975. It was used on one other occasion, the last, when Regazzoni failed to finish at Mante Carlo.

Engine: rear flat 12. Displacement: 2991,8 cc. Bore and stroke: 80x49,6 mm. Compression ratio: 11,5:1. Power: 495 bhp at 12.500 rpm. Valve gear: 4 valves per cylinder, dohc. Fuel system: Lucas injection. Ignition: single, capacitive ignition (AEC 104) Magneti Marelli. Gearbox: 5 speeds + reverse inside the wheelbase. Brakes: Lockheed discs and calipers (inboard rear). Frame: unitized monocoque, rivetted aluminium panels, rectangular section, ladder steel tubing. Suspension, front: twin wishbones, inboard spring-dampers. Suspension, rear: single upper lateral link, reversed lower wishbone, single trailing link, outboard spring dampers. Tracks: 1510 mm (front), 1530 mm (rear). Wheelbase: 2518 mm. Weight: 575 kg (dry)

312 T2

The car of 1976. The year of Niki Lauda's terrible accident at the Nürburgring. The year of the world title which the Austrian lost by only one point, after the last race in Japan. The year of controversy therefore. But Ferrari was still right up there: competitive as ever. 1976 was the year of the T2. It was not particularly different from its predecessor. But the body was about 20 kilos lighter and the air intake above the roll bar had disappeared. Niki Lauda and Clay Regazzoni had their contracts renewed but there was a change of race manager with Daniele Audetto coming in to replace Luca di Montezemolo. The T2 first appeared on the track in a non-title race when Niki Lauda drove it in the Race of Champions at Brands Hatch on the 14th of March. The Austrian was in the third row alongside Jody Scheckter in the Tyrrell. The car stopped on the 17th lap with a broken brake pipe.

The world championship debut was in Spain on the 2nd of May. There was a good deal of argument on the eve of the race. Niki Lauda was unwell. The effects of an unusual accident were still giving him pain. He

had fractured two ribs, "playing" with a tractor. They fixed him up and pronounced him fit to practice and to race. Despite the fact that he was clearly handicapped, the Austrian made the second best time and came second behind winner James Hunt in the McLaren.

The first victory for the "T2" came in Belgium. It was a Ferrari double for Lauda and Regazzoni in that order. Then it was Lauda again at Monaco. Regazzoni was unlucky, he was betrayed by an oil slick and had to withdraw. Lauda was third in Sweden, Regazzoni sixth. In France, the Austrian tried out the rear suspension with the de Dion axle in practice. The movable appendages set ahead of the front wheels were judged irregular. In the race, Ferrari suffered a sensational setback: the engines of both cars broke down. McLaren won again in England. The appeal against Hunt, who had taken part in the

second start of the Grand Prix without having any right to do so, was accepted by the FIA and Lauda found himself with an extra win. Regazzoni's run of bad luck continued however and he did not finish at Brands Hatch.

Then came the Nrburgring and the terrible accident. The T2 flew and burst into flames. For several days Lauda hung between life and death until suddenly he rallied. The recovery was rapid and six weeks later he showed up at Monza, still bandaged, still suffering, but determined to race. In the meantime Ferrari had deserted the Austrian Grand Prix and Regazzoni had gone to Holland alone. He came second. Carlos Reutemann was also at Monza in a third Ferrari. He had been engaged in case of a slow recovery on Lauda's part. Reutemann's presence was an embarrassment not so much for Lauda, who took fourth place—thus adding three points to his lead over Hunt (DNF)—but for Clay Regazzoni, whose intuition told him that his position at Ferrari was in danger.

Ferrari looked like it was on the way to another world title. But things went wrong. Hunt won in Canada and at Watkins Glen.

Engine: rear flat 12. Displacement: 2991,8 cc. Bore and stroke: 80x49,6 mm. Compression ratio: 11,5:1. Power: 500 bhp at 12.200 rpm. Valve gear: 4 valves per cylinder, dohc. Fuel system: Lucas injection. Ignition: single, capacitive ignition (AEC 104) Magneti Marelli. Gearbox: 5 speeds + reverse, inside the wheelbase. Brakes: Brembo ventilated discs (rear inboard), Lockheed calipers. Frame: unitized monocoque, rivetted aluminium panels, light alloy structure. Suspension, front: unequal length A-arms, inboard spring-dampers. Suspension, rear: single upper lateral link, reversed lower wishbones, single trailing link, outboard spring dampers. Tracks: 1405 mm (front), 1430 mm (rear). Wheelbase: 2560 mm. Weight: 578 kg (dry).

The last event was in Japan. Lauda still had a three point lead over Hunt. Then the Fuji circuit was hit by a tremendous deluge. The race was on just the same, but at the end of the second lap Lauda was already in the pits. An electrical failure? No, the Austrian did not want to carry on and so Hunt was the champion by one point. It was a sensation and controversy raged. Lauda silenced his critics when he took his second world title, and

Ferrari's eighth, in the T2 in 1977. Then came the unexpected split and the Austrian went off to Brabham-Alfa, but he did not race in the last two Grand Prix of the season. A little French Canadian made his appearance on the Formula 1 scene. His name was Gilles Villeneuve. The T2 raced in the first two Grand Prix of 1978 as well, and it scored an excellent victory in Brazil. The T2's score is as follows: eight wins out of 31 races, 12 second places, five pole positions. The T3 took over as from the South African Grand Prix of the 4th March 1978. The T2 shown in these pages is the one which made its debut with Niki Lauda at the 1975 Race of Champions. Then it was raced by Regazzoni in Spain (11th), in Belgium (2nd), and in Germany (9th), and finally by Reutemann at Monza (9th).

312 T3

Aerodynamic research in the wind tunnel. The driver surrounded by a safety cell cockpit: Gilles Villeneuve knew something about that. A time of ground effect and turbos, which Renault brought back to Formula 1. At Ferrari the evolution of the T continued in the wake of Lauda's eighth world championship win. There was considerable technical ferment in Formula 1 in 1977. Aerodynamic research was a priority and the wind tunnels were going flat out. Radial tyres. And above all, the return of the supercharger. This was thanks to the level of development reached by the "turbo", and more knowledge regarding combustion and fuels.

The Renault, with its turbo and its Michelin radials, made its debut at Silverstone on the 16th July 1977.

Gilles Villeneuve was also on his F1 debut in the McLaren. 1978 was just as full of technical innovation. Colin Chapman invented the "wing-car" which gave Mario Andretti his first and only F1 world title (the only American to do so apart from Phil Hill). Carlo Chiti produced the rear suction fan (tried before on the Chaparral) and fitted it to the Brabham-Alfa with which Niki Lauda won the Swedish Grand Prix. A win which was never cancelled, despite the subsequent ban on the fan. All the teams decided to go with the flow and the miniskirt system was universally copied. Ferrari, and Mauro Forghieri in particular, looked for ground effect in a different way.

"The T3,'explained Forghieri', is a car which did not use the miniskirts but which offered the ground a highly elevated surface. We realized that by both widening and applying a certain angulation to the surface presented to the ground we obtained relatively efficient depressions which increased the negative lift of the car or reduced positive lift according to how you want to look at it."

But there were important novelties at Ferrari too. Above all, there was the agreement with Michelin. The passage from the T2 to the T3 was strongly influenced by the adoption of radial tyres. Then each structural group making up the car was made independent of the others. This meant each sector could be developed separately without one influencing the other. The monocoque was a new design. The front suspension had a smaller spring-damper assembly which was set vertically. The "cockpit-cell" came into being; it was capable of absorbing impacts and

consequent deformation in the case of accidents.
Ronnie Peterson's death following the Monza accident, had underlined the structural weakness of the Lotus and this was a warning for everyone. Ferrari was universally recognized as the safest car of all as Gilles Villeneuve's shunt was to prove. Finally, aerodynamic research was refined even further with the use of the Pininfarina and Fiat wind tunnels. It is worth remembering that although Fiat had become a 50 per cent partner in Ferrari Auto in 1969, complete power of decision was left in the hands of the racing department.
The 12-cylinder engine reached 510 bhp and the weight was 580 kilogrammes.

The T3 introduced in the November of 1977 following Lauda's success and the unexpected "divorce" which then ensued, had a brief life. It was used from March '78 to February '79.
It raced in 16 Grands Prix overall and won four of them (three with Reutemann, one with Villeneuve). The car shown in these pages, is owned by an Italian collector. It was raced by Carlos Reutemann in 1978 in South Africa (DNF), in Belgium (3rd), in Spain (DNF), in Gt. Britain (1st), in Germany (DNF). In 1979, with this same model, Gilles Villeneuve won the Race of Champions, on the 15th of April at Brands Hatch, a race which is not valid for the world championship.

Engine: rear flat 12. Displacement: 2991,8 cc. Bore and stroke: 80x49,6 mm. Compression ratio: 11,5:1. Power: 510 bhp at 12.200 rpm. Valve gear: 4 valves per cylinder, dohc. Fuel system: Lucas injection. Ignition: single, capacitive ignition (AEC 104) Magneti Marelli. Gearbox: 5 speeds + reverse, inside the wheelbase. Brakes: Brembo ventilated discs (rear inboard), Lockheed calipers. Frame: unitized monocoque, rivetted aluminium panels, light alloy structure. Suspension, front: unequal length A-arms, inboard spring-dampers. Suspension, rear: unequal length A-arms, upper link, upper radius arm, lower wishbones, radius arm. Tracks: 1620 mm (front), 1585 mm (rear). Wheelbase: 2560 mm. Weight: 580 kg (dry).

312 T3

Debut in south Africa. Used from March '78 to February '79. Sixteen Grand Prix: Four wins. Three with Carlos Reutemann, one with Gilles Villeneuve. During the year, tyre problems plus some errors on Reutemann's part thwarted Ferrari's attempt to score a second championship success. The T3 made its debut at the Kyalami circuit where the third event in the championship calendar took place on the 4th of March 1978. Reutemann was fresh from his triumph in Rio but Gilles Villeneuve was ahead of him on the starting grid. The Canadian was in the fourth row and the Argentinian in the fifth. While the radial tyres fitted to Reutemann's T2 in Brazil had been winners, they had been found to be incompatible with the front suspension of the T3. It was

an unlucky race and Villeneuve's engine broke down on the 57th lap. Soon afterwards Reutemann went playing due to the oil which his teammate's car had left on the track.

In the US West Grand Prix at Long Beach the T3s started in the first row with Reutemann in pole position. The gap between the two ferraristi was only two tenths of a second. The race was full of electrifying moments. At the end of the first straight Reutemann was leading but then at the corner he was nudged by Andretti and Watson. Villeneuve took over the lead. Only nine months had gone by since his Formula 1 debut and six since he had joined Ferrari. Gilles seemed sure to win, but as he was overtaking Regazzoni on the 38th lap he had an accident which put him out of the race.

After that, Reutemann's race went smoothly as he drove the T3 to its first win. The victory also took him to the top of the points table, a position he shared with Andretti (Lotus). The Argentinian was faster than Villeneuve again during practice for the Monaco Grand Prix. He took pole position while the Canadian was back in the fourth row. Reutemann got off to a bad start and was bumped by Lauda before an enforced visit to the pits for a tyre change. He had lost a lot of ground but his fightback was one of the truly memorable ones. He finished eighth. Villeneuve failed to finish once more. Reutemann was in the front row again at Zolder, this time with the second best time behind Andretti. Villeneuve was in the second row. Again the Argentinian made a poor start and finished in third place. Villeneuve was fourth. The two Lotuses were in the front row, with Andretti and Peterson. Reutemann recorded the third best time and Villeneuve the fifth. Inexplicable tyre problems made it a race to forget for Ferrari. Reutemann went off the track (not the fault of the tyres on this occasion) and Villeneuve had to visit the pits twice for a tyre change and could not manage better than tenth place. In Sweden Lauda's "sucker" won. The Ferraris, back in the fourth row, did not seem to be in contention and in fact Villeneuve came ninth and Reutemann tenth. When the gadget on the Brabham was banned, Lotus got back in the driving seat. Andretti won the French GP in grand style. Reutemann made the fastest lap but had to change tyres a good five times. He came in eighteenth, five laps behind. Villeneuve's 12th place was a little better. The Lotuses broke down in England

and Reutemann was first past the post after a thrilling duel with Lauda. Villeneuve dropped out with a broken axle shaft. In Germany and Austria, first Andretti and then Peterson sorted them all out. At Hockenheim Reutemann dropped out and Villeneuve was only eighth. At Zeltweg, Reutemann was disqualified and Villeneuve's third place got him on to the podium at last. Andretti won again in Holland as Ferrari came sixth and seventh with Villeneuve and Reutemann. Then Ronnie Peterson died at Monza. Lauda won that day, but Andretti became world champion. A bitter title, as the American was to say. Reutemann was third and Villeneuve seventh. It was all Ferrari at the end of the season, as experimentation continued on the ground effect T3. Reutemann won at Watkins Glen and Villeneuve, who did not finish in the US, won in Canada. This was the likeable Canadian's first GP win. Ferrari's success was complete with Reutemann's third place. The car shown in these pages was driven by Gilles Villeneuve in all the championship events from Long Beach onwards, with the exception of the British and German Grand Prix. Still with Villeneuve, it came fifth in the '79 Brazilian Grand Prix.

Engine: rear flat 12. Displacement: 2991,8 cc. Bore and stroke: 80x49,6 mm. Compression ratio: 11,5:1. Power: 510 bhp at 12.200 rpm. Valve gear: 4 valves per cylinder, dohc. Fuel system: Lucas injection. Ignition: single plug, capacitive ignition (AEC 104) Magneti Marelli. Gearbox: 5 speeds + reverse, inside the wheelbase. Brakes: Brembo ventilated discs (rear inboard), Lockheed calipers. Frame: unitized monocoque, rivetted aluminium panels, light alloy structure. Suspension, front: unequal length A-arms, inboard spring-dampers. Suspension, rear: unequal A-arms, upper link, upper radius arm, lower wishbone. Tracks: 1620 mm (front), 1585 mm (rear). Wheelbase: 2560 mm. Weight: 590 kg (dry).

312 T4

The car which won the ninth world title for Ferrari, with Jody Scheckter on his debut in Maranello red. A winning debut in the South African Grand Prix. Total: five wins, numerous placings. It was the last win for a Ferrari in the drivers' championship.

The ugliest—the word is Ferrari's—but the most efficient of the T series. Miniskirts. "Integral" ground effect. Almost central driving position. Controls which allowed the driver to adjust the suspension. Few modifications during the season confirmed its validity: double calipers on all four discs; new exhausts and new suspension; the spoiler set further up. While experimentation with the new turbo continued at Renault, and while the Ford Cosworth was still in good form, the Ferrari T4 was walking away with the marque's ninth, and so far, most recent, world title. The season began with a change in the ranks of the drivers: Villeneuve stayed, Reutemann left and Scheckter arrived. The South African driver immediately announced that he had joined Ferrari in order to win the world title. Villeneuve, who also nurtured legitimate ambitions, created no problems. The pair were friends. Marco Piccini, manager responsible for racing since the beginning of '78, was confirmed.

Engine: rear flat 12. Displacement: 2991,8 cc. Bore and stroke: 80x49,6 mm (1958). Compression ratio: 11,5:1. Power: 515 bhp at 12.300 rpm. Valve gear: 4 valves per cylinder, dohc. Fuel system: Lucas injection. Ignition: single, capacitive ignition (AEC 104) Magneti Marelli. Gearbox: 5 speeds + reverse inside the wheelbase. Brakes: Brembo ventilated discs (rear inboard), Lockheed calipers. Frame: unitized monocoque, rivetted aluminium panels, light alloy structure. Suspension, front: unequal length A-arms, inboard spring-dampers. Suspension, rear: unequal length A-arms, upper link, upper radius arm, lower wishbones. Tracks: 1700 mm (front), 1600 mm (rear). Wheelbase: 2700 mm. Weight: 590 kg (dry).

The T4 debuted in the South African GP, the third appointment on the world championship calendar. Villeneuve and Scheckter made it a one-two right away. The same thing happened at Long Beach. The Ferraris were in command. Ligier and Lotus were their most determined rivals. Villeneuve was leading the world rankings ahead of Lafitte and Scheckter. In Spain the Canadian was left without brakes and first gear. This caused him all sorts of problems and he came in seventh with no points. His teammate came fourth and from Belgium onwards the balance swung in favour of Scheckter. Jody won that race but Villeneuve was the star of the show. Held up in the pits while they changed the front end, Gilles embarked on a spectacular fight back which took him to third place. He ran out of petrol 300 metres from the finish, but he came seventh all the same. But he scored no points in this Grand Prix either. Scheckter won again in Monaco to rack up Ferrari's fourth win on the Monegasque circuit. Villeneuve, who had been in second place, withdrew with transmission trouble. That left Scheckter alone at the top of the rankings. The progress of the race, with both Ferraris leading without attacking each other, shows that the team was united and devoid of excessive rivalry. The credit for this goes to Villeneuve. Scheckter had a setback in France and took no points. The Dijon event was a historic Grand Prix for two reasons: it was Renault's first victory there and the first victory for their turbo blown engine. There was also a great duel between Villeneuve and Arnoux, the former getting the better of his opponent to arrive within four points of his teammate in the world rankings. All was yet possible. Scheckter picked up two points at Silverstone for his fifth place while Villeneuve did not finish although he was awarded fourteenth place just the same. Now it was the Williams which represented the biggest danger and not the Ligier. The Williams scored four consecutive wins: Regazzoni won at Silverstone, Jones at Hockenheim, Zeltweg and Zandvoort. Scheckter was fourth in Germany and Austria and picked up another six points. Then he came second at Zandvoort on a day of powerful emotions: particularly Villeneuve's battle with Jones and his desperate but futile attempt to get back to the pits on three wheels. Then there was Scheckter's climb from 19th to 2nd place within 25 laps. Monza saw a Ferrari double with Scheckter's win clinching the world title. The Canadian's second place confirmed his sense of discipline. The end of the season was all Villeneuve, runner-up in Canada and victor at Watkins Glen. He ended the season right behind Scheckter. The T4 seen here is the property of Gilles Villeneuve's Italian sponsor. It is the car in which the Canadian raced in 1979 at the French, German, Austrian, Dutch, Canadian and Eastern US Grand Prix.

312 T5

The swan song, a bitter one unfortunately, of Mauro Forghieri's 12-cylinder boxer. Tyre and engine problems. Jody Scheckter announces his retirement from racing well in advance. A year in decline. No wins. But the new Ferrari turbo was on the way.

The Fisa-Foca war. Regazzoni's accident, and the retirement of the new world champion, Jody Scheckter. A holocaust of engines at Ferrari. The swan song of the 12-cylinder boxer. The preparation of the new Ferrari turbo. Non stop action, as they say.

Ferrari began the championship with the new car in the line-up. In the past, they had always sent the old models to the South American events. Tradition had it that a winning car was always followed by a loser (with the exception of that legendary 500 with which Alberto Ascari won two straight world championships in '52 and '53). This was the case with the T5. The car's poor effectiveness was due to a series of circumstances which drove Enzo Ferrari to declare that the season had not been merely "so-so" but "totally negative".

Tyre problems. Ferrari put it like this at the end of the season; "We reached the conclusion that if the T5 had had tyres like those used by the opposition it could have been among the points quite often". Engine problems: "In Brazil 'said Ferrari again' where Villeneuve could have had a magnificent race, we began the awful business of pressurizing seven engines, on account of a faulty front gasket on the water pump in the distribution which had us going mad before we spotted it, and two engines which had been dismantled because of their frequent failures and inexplicable power loss. We finally discovered that the carbon fibre material used for the body was brushing against the wires which took current to the plugs which were promptly discharging against the bodywork."

Effort was concentrated on the development of the turbo. "I believe that the turbo blown engine is the engine of the future. Today's aspirated engine can produce 170 bhp per litre, 175 at the most. All our engines develop 510/515 bhp. It will be difficult to exceed this ceiling. On the other hand, I am sure that a 1500 cc turbo blown engine could develop as much as 600 bhp."

An unmotivated driver: Scheckter. "A champion's career follows a predestined curve. When a man becomes world champion he becomes above all a public relations man, distracted by a thousand concerns. He can no longer concentrate on racing and racing is no longer his major objective", said Ferrari.

Even though the T5 was a natural development of the T4, it did possess some novel features like new, narrower heads and a different geometry for the front suspension. It had better aerodynamic penetration too. Despite this, basic problems cropped up immediately and the car, which should have been better, was not. Apart from the engine problems, the tyre to car relationship was crucial. Michelin, busy defending itself from Goodyear, who had been supplying an extremely competitive tyre from Long Beach onwards, was reserving most of its efforts for Renault. But the solutions adopted for the French manufacturer were not found to be as effective for the Maranello cars.

The T5 did not manage to win a Grand Prix. It made 8 points in all, 6 with Villeneuve, 2 with Scheckter. The glorious life of the 12-cylinder boxer came to an end with the T5. It had won 37 out of 158 races.

These pages show the T5 which belongs to an Italian collector. This model was frequently used in practice. For example, in Argentina, Brazil, France and Spain, where the Fisa-Foca war broke out. Then it took part in three races. In Austria, Scheckter started in the second last row. There were more than five seconds between his Ferrari and Arnoux's Renault in pole position. It came thirteenth in the race. Scheckter failed to qualify in Canada and the car was entrusted to Velleneuve who drove it to fifth place. Finally in the Eastern US Grand Prix, at Watkins Glen, Scheckter was back to record the second slowest time in practice. He was eleventh in the race, which was to be the last for him and the last for the T5.

Engine: rear flat 12. Displacement: 2991,8 cc. Bore and stroke: 80x49,6 mm (1958). Compression ratio: 11,5:1. Power: 515 bhp at 12.200 rpm. Valve gear: 4 valves per cylinder, dohc. Fuel system: Lucas injection. Ignition: single, capacitive ignition (AEC 104) Magneti Marelli. Gearbox: 5 speeds + reverse, inside the wheelbase. Brakes: Brembo ventilated discs (rear inboard), Lockheed calipers. Frame: unitized monocoque, rivetted aluminium panels, light alloy structure. Suspension, front: unequal length A-arms, double wishbones, inboard spring-dampers. Suspension, rear: unequal lenght A-arms, upper link, upper radius arm, lower wishbones. Tracks: 1750 mm (front), 1625 mm (rear). Wheelbase: 2700 mm. Weight: 595 kg (dry).

312 T5

An unhappy start for this car in the first three Grand Prix of the season. Neither Villeneuve nor Scheckter managed to finish. Ferrari took part in the '80 championship with six frames from the T5 series.

Villeneuve's crash at Imola demonstrated the level of safety reached by this car. The T5 took part in the world championship with six frames ranging from the 042 to the 048 (but without the 047). The 042 car picked up three consecutive withdrawals: engine failure in Argentina and Brazil, with Jody Scheckter, and a broken axle shaft in South Africa with Gilles Villeneuve. It was not used again. No T5 managed to finish in the first three Grand Prix of the season. The suspension on Gilles Villeneuve's 043 broke in Buenos Aires and then the accelerator on his 045 let him down in Brazil. Scheckter's 046 suffered engine failure in South Africa but the same driver scored the first championship points at Long Beach. With the same frame, the South African came eighth

in Belgium, withdrew at Monaco, practiced but did not race in Spain (only the cars adhering to the constructor's association took part). Then he came 12th in France, 10th in England, and 13th in Germany. That was the 046's last race. Villeneuve drove the 043 in Austria and at Watkins Glen, and Scheckter took it to Imola which was hosting the Italian Grand Prix that year. The 044 with Scheckter driving was 13th in Austria and 11th at Watkins Glen. Villeneuve achieved a better placing when he came fifth in Canada. As well as racing in Brazil, the 045 was in the line-up (with Villeneuve) at Long Beach (DNF) and Mante Carlo (fifth). The 048 took part in three races:

Villeneuve failed to finish at Brands Hatch, came sixth at Hockenheim, and at Imola he dropped out after an accident. Evidence of the Ferrari's robustness was provided at the Santerno circuit. On the fifth lap, at the Tosa corner, one of Villeneuve's tyres blew out. The Canadian slammed into the safety fence at about 290 kph. The impact was extremely violent but the driver climbed out of the cockpit safe and sound. Shocked yes, but all in one piece. Ferrari said: "An accident like the one at Imola demonstrates that with 608-612 kilos you can build an extremely safe car in which the `cell' containing the driver will remain intact even after 270-280 kph impacts. Ferrari has beaten no records this year but we believe we have shown many people that drivers' lives can be saved by not cutting corners on the weight when building cars." The T5's decline as the year went on could be seen more clearly by its performance in practice. The fourth and sixth rows in Argentina. The

second and fourth in Brazil. The fifth in South Africa and the fifth and eighth at Long Beach. Sixth and seventh in Belgium and third and ninth at Monaco. Up to this point, the results were reasonable if not spectacular, but as from the French Grand Prix, Ferrari slid right to the back of the grid on the fast European circuits. The ninth and tenth row in France. Tenth and twelfth in Great Britain and eighth and eleventh in Germany and Austria. Things seemed to improve in Holland (fourth and sixth row) and Imola (fourth and eighth). But the T5 picked up the worst results of the season in the last two races. In Canada Scheckter did not even qualify while Villeneuve could only make the back row. Villeneuve started in the eighth row at Watkins Glen but only Jan Lammers was behind Scheckter.
It is difficult to say how much

Engine: mid-rear flat 12. Displacement: 2991,8 cc. Bore and stroke: 80x49,6 mm. Compression ratio: 11,5:1. Power: 515 bhp at 12.200 rpm. Valve gear: 4 valves per cylinder, dohc. Fuel system: Lucas injection. Ignition: single, capacitive discharge ignition (AEC 104) Magneti Marelli. Gearbox: 5 speeds + reverse, inside the wheelbase. Brakes: Brembo ventilated discs (rear inboard), Lockheed calipers. Frame: unitized monocoque, rivetted aluminium panels, light alloy structure. Suspension, front: unequal length A-arms, inboard spring-dampers. Suspension, rear: unequal lenght A-arms, upper link, upper radius arm, lower wishbone. Tracks: 1750 mm (front), 1625 mm (rear). Wheelbase: 2700 mm. Weight: 595 kg (dry).

Scheckter's poor motivation was due to his decision to retire, announced just after the British Grand Prix. From Hockenheim to Watkins Glen, Villeneuve had always been the fastest in practice, but the

difference between the Canadian driver—always considered one of the fastest and boldest on the circuit— and Jody Scheckter was always minimal. With some rare exceptions, both of them started well back on the quid most of the time and this would seem to point to a progressive falling away of the car's ability to compete, rather than a lack of commitment on the drivers' part.

126 C4

The Ferrari turbo, a 120° V6 with KKK turbos, had been racing since 1981. It already held a record: the first win with Villeneuve at Monaco a mere two and a half months after its debut. Since then, Gilles had died and Pironi was injured. An Italian driver, Alboreto, returned. The C4 was a disappointment for drivers and technicians.

The 126 CK was born in 1981. The C stands for *"Compressore"*, and the K refers to the KKK turbosuperchargers. In September of 1980, Ferrari said: "The Turbo is not derived from the T5. In the light of certain advanced features I could say that it is a completely new car. Just consider the engine design which has the exhausts in the

middle and the intake where the exhausts were, or the computerized fuel feed and the many other variations". The car had just made its debut in practice for the Italian grand Prix at Imola. But the 126 also had something "old" inside it: the engine. The 120° V6 used by Ferrari to power the 156 F1 in 1961, the engine which had taken Phil Hill to world championship glory, was exactly the same as the "new" 6-cylinder unit apart from variations in the bore and stroke and compression ratio.

Various types of turbocharger were tried out on the engine, which was in preparation by the summer of '79: the German KKK (Kuhnle, Kopp, and Kausch), the

American Garrett and the Brown Boveri Comprex. Enzo Ferrari explained: "We have opted for the KKK for the moment because we had prepared things specially for it, but we are still carrying on research with the Comprex. From a performance point of view the two KKK turbos undoubtedly offer notable power. The Comprex on the other hand offers exceptionally good response times. The problem regarding `turbo lag' no longer exist and we have a fast response, like you get with an aspirated engine. There are problems regarding the cooling of the inducted air, because it should not be inducted at a temperature in excess of 60 degrees. Now we have new heat exchangers, which were the fruit of work carried out on our behalf at the Fiat research centre and which we ourselves partially constructed. We have to try out all these things."

Testing was carried out with the KKK for a while and also with the Comprex (in the latter case the 126 also received the CX cypher).

In the end they chose the KKK. Ferrari was ready for the off in the 1981 championship with 560 bhp at 11500 rpm.

Fisa and Foca were still at war and only the Foca teams took part in the South African GP. Then the race was annulled. Finally an armistice was signed. The mobile miniskirts disappeared but the rigid lateral skirts remained. Then someone (Gordon Murray of Brabham) invented a gadget with which the

Engine: mid-rear 120° V-6. Displacement: 1496,4 cc. Bore and stroke: 81x48,4 mm (1958). Compression ratio: 6,7:1. Power: 660 bhp at 11.000 rpm (racing), 800 bhp at 11.000 rpm (testing). Valve gear: 4 valves per cylinder, dohc. Fuel system: 2 central top KKK turbos, Lucas-Ferrari injection or Weber-Marelli digital electronic Emulsistem. Ignition: single plug, Magneti Marelli, capacitive discharge ignition. Gearbox: 5 speeds + reverse, inside the wheelbase. Brakes: cast iron or carbon discs (outboard), Brembo calipers. Frame: monocoque in composite materials (Kevlar and carbon fiber). Suspension, front: double wishbones, pull-rod suspension control. Suspension, rear: twin wishbones, pull-rod suspension control. Tracks: 1768,4 mm (front), 1680,2 mm (rear). Wheelbase: 2600 mm. Weight: 540 kg (dry).

driver could lower the car's suspension during the race (in breach of the rules) and return to a height of 60 mm before the technical checks. Ferrari was late in falling into line with this solution but it won two Grand Prix just the same when Gilles Villeneuve took Monaco and Spain. Two consecutive wins in what was the debut season for

the Ferrari turbo was most surprising and the technical staff at Maranello were justly proud. But although the car had a very competitive engine, it was less so regarding the frame. A technical expert in composite materials, Harvey Postlethwaite, came to Ferrari from England. In the meantime the BMW turbo was taking its first steps. The 126 C2

83

arrived in 1982. A composite monocoque powered by an engine with highly advanced electronic systems and water injection. 580 bhp at 11000 rpm. The tyres were no longer Michelin, but Goodyear. A winning car, it was dogged by ill luck. Ferrari scored a double at Imola where Pironi overtook Villeneuve towards the end causing a violent argument between the two drivers. Villeneuve died in Belgium. Prioni seemed on track for the

championship. He won in Holland, came second in England and third in France. But he had a serious accident while practising for the German GP and the Frenchman's career was over. The 126 C2 was to score its third victory right there in Germany with Patrick Tambay. In 1983 the lateral skirts disappeared and the flat bottoms arrived. Ferrari faced the first part of the season with a standby car, the C2B, which nevertheless won at San Marino with Tambay

and in Canada with Arnoux. The C3 took the field after the English GP. It was an even more avant garde car, with a Kevlar and carbon fibre frame plus electronic injection. The engine developed 600 bhp at 10500 rpm and it won twice with Réne Arnoux in Germany and Holland.

The C4 finally arrived in 1984. It was arrow shaped with a lighter body, engine, and gearbox-differential. It debuted in the Brazilian Grand Prix and showed itself competitive on mixed tracks, though it was less so on purely fast tracks. Alboreto's win in Belgium was the only one.

These pages show the car with which Michele Alboreto raced in Brazil (DNF), South Africa (12th) and Monaco (7th). It was used as a `muletto' at Zolder, Imola, Dijon, Hockenheim, Monza, Brands Hatch, and Estoril. In January 1985 it was used in practice at the Paul Ricard and the Estoril.

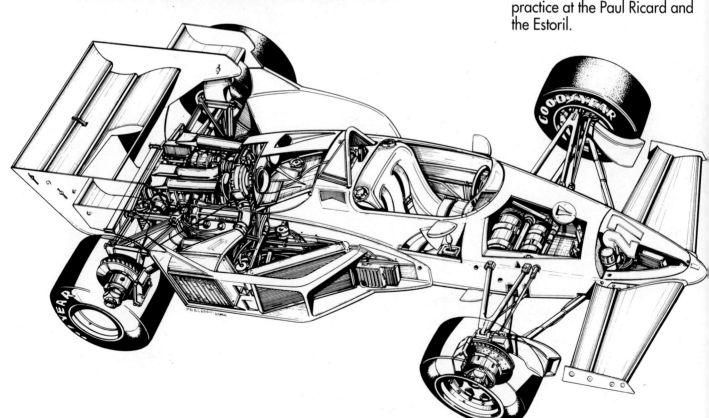

126 C4

Maximum attention paid to consumption. New injection systems. Redesigned engine. Although it should have been competitive, the C4 did not obtain any important results. Problems with tyres, suspension and injection held back performance. Only one victory, with Alboreto.

The C4 engine was widely redesigned. In 1984 a great deal of attention was being paid to fuel consumption. New completely computerized electronically controlled injection systems arose. And an Italian driver joined Ferrari for the first time since Merzario's time, eleven years before: Michele Alboreto. His partner was René Arnoux.

In the Brazilian Grand Prix, the first event on the championship calendar, Alboreto recorded the second best time, Arnoux the tenth. Neither of the two got to the finish. Alboreto dropped out with a broken front brake caliper and Arnoux with battery failure.

Prost won in the McLaren. This was the first win for the TAG-Porsche turbo blown engine, seven months after its debut. The Ferrari record of a victory (Monaco, 1981) only two months after the championship debut of its turbo engine still stands. Arnoux withdrew again in South

came fourth again in Monaco, then fifth in Canada, before failing to finish in Detroit. He managed second place in the Dallas GP despite having to start in the last row due to an error on the grid. Then he came sixth in England and Germany, seventh in Austria, where the wrong

the petrol pump broke down, the heat exchanger split at Detroit, and he crashed at Dallas. After a fifth place in England, he failed to finish again in Germany due to a broken distributor cap. There was a third place in Austria, but a broken turbocharger forced his withdrawal in Holland. The last

Africa, this time with a breakdown in the electronic control module, while Alboreto was knocked out of contention by vapour lock in the fuel system after only twelve laps. Ferrari scored its only Grand Prix victory of the season in Belgium where Alboreto was first across the line after starting in pole position. Arnoux, who also started in the first row, came third. The car really seemed to be among the most competitive, but a series of problems—tyres, suspension, injection—led to a poor series of results. At the San Marino GP Alboreto had to withdraw with a broken exhaust but Arnoux, despite a similar problem, managed to come second. Alboreto failed to finish again in France (engine), while Arnoux was fourth despite another break in the exhaust. The Frenchman

choice of tyres at the start cost time later. He did not finish in Holland owing to trouble with the electrics and at Monza the gearbox failed. A fifth place followed at the Grand Prix d'Europe at the Nürburgring, and then a ninth in Portugal. After a seventh place at Monaco, Alboreto endured a worrying series of withdrawals: in Holland

three Grands Prix went better for Alboreto and Ferrari with two seconds (at Monza and the Nürburgring) and a fourth in Portugal.
From the Austrian GP onwards the car was 130 mm longer and the suspension was also modified. An "M" was added to the C4 to indicate the modifications made to the frame.

Engine: mid-rear 90° V-6. Displacement: 1496,4 cc. Bore and stroke: 81x48,4 mm. Compression ratio: 8:1. Power: 880 bhp at 11.500 rpm (racing), 930 bhp at 11.500 rpm (testing). Valve gear: 4 valves per cylinder, dohc. Fuel system: 2 lateral Garrett turbos, Weber-Marelli electronic digital injection, double injectors. Ignition: single plug, Magneti Marelli electrostatic ignition. Gearbox: 6 speeds + reverse, overhanging longitudinal rear. Brakes: ventilated carbon discs (outboard), Brembo calipers. Frame: monocoque in composite materials (Kevlar and carbon fibre). Suspension, front: unequal length A-arms, pull-rod suspension control. Suspension, rear: twin wishbones, pull-rod suspension control. Tracks: 1791 mm (front), 1673 mm (rear). Wheelbase: 2800 mm. Weight: 542 kg (dry).

The Ferrari drivers finished the championship with half of Lauda's points score. The Austrian took his third world title by half a point from Prost. In the course of the season, Mauro Forghieri's engine had come under fire from the press. At the press conference (29th of August) held on the eve of the Italian Grand Prix, Enzo Ferrari said: "If I had to race at Mante Carlo, Detroit or Dallas, I would build the C4 again, but I certainly wouldn't if I had to go to Brands Hatch or Zeltweg." In a few words, the C4 was just right for the street circuits, but it was not competitive on the fast tracks. It was to be Forghieri's last season in any case, and he was given another job within Ferrari. These pages show the car with which Arnoux raced in Brazil, South Africa, Belgium and Imola, and Alboreto raced in Germany, Austria and Holland.

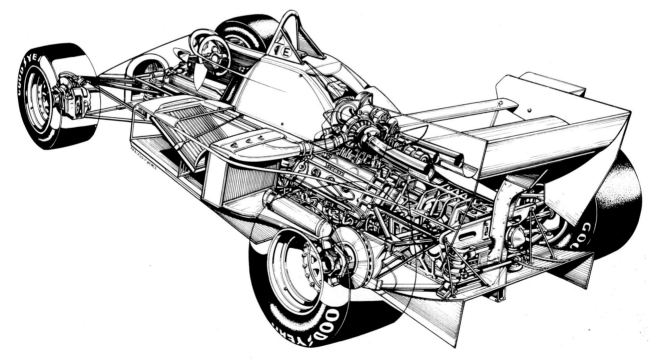

F1-87

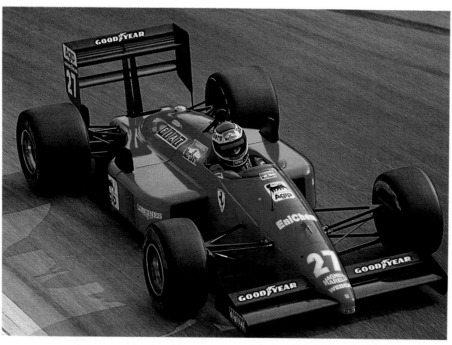

Designed by Gustav Brunner, developed by John Barnard. The engine was still the same: a 6-cylinder. But the inclination had been reduced to 90°. It amassed twenty retirements: eleven with Alboreto, nine with Berger. But Ferrari was back at the top by the end of the year. Berger won in Japan and Australia.
The 156 was in the 1985 line-up. The cypher was the same as that of the car which won the world title with Phil Hill. The engine delivered 780 bph at 11000 rpm. After the Brazilian Grand Prix, Arnoux was replaced by the Swede Johnasson. Michele Alboreto won the Canadian and the German Grand Prix in the 156.

It took six high placings (four with Alboreto, two with Johansson) and failed to finish eleven times. Until the Dutch Grand Prix, Alboreto had seemed on course for the title. Then the 156 started to suffer from notable loss of power. There were problems with the frame and some of the engine accessories. Prost took the title in the McLaren.
The F1-86 arrived in 1986 and Alboreto and Johansson were kept on. It was a very disappointing season. 15 withdrawals over all, no wins, and the best result was Alboreto's second place in Austria. Prost won his second world championship. McLaren

was on its third victory running. There was a technical change in 1987. The F1-87 was designed by the Austrian, Gustav Brunner, who left Ferrari when the new technical manager arrived. This was John Barnard, the man who had taken McLaren to the top. The F1-87 had a reduced frontal section and it was decided to refit the longitudinal gearbox, but the real novelty was the engine. It was still a six cylinder, but the angle was at 90 instead of 120 degrees. The Austrian driver, Berger, replaced Johansson. Williams-Honda and McLaren-Porsche dominated almost the entire season. The Ferrari F1-87 was back at the top for the last two events with Berger winning in Japan and Australia. Ferrari had a double in that last race, with a second place for Alboreto. Two high notes to put an end to an unhappy season. The statistics are significant: the F1-87 racked up 20 withdrawals (11 with Alboreto, who suffered 10 in a row; 9 with Berger) and only two second places (one for each driver). At the end of the season, Enzo Ferrari commented: "Everybody did his bit. By the time Barnard joined Ferrari Brunner had already made the body and it's clear that the others added what they thought it was right to add. In conclusion, if I had to compile a

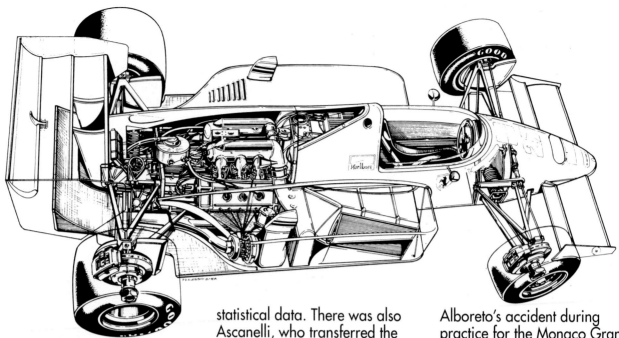

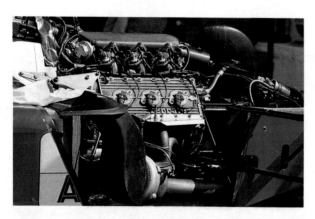

statistical data. There was also Ascanelli, who transferred the wind tunnel data to the car. Nor must we forget Nardon and the others who contributed to its preparation. I repeat, the car was the result of teamwork."

Mansell was the favourite for the world title. But it was to be his teammate, Nelson Piquet, who ran out the winner. The F1-87 which is shown in these pages bears chassis number 95.

This was the first body built for this new model and it was used for winter testing and as a "*muletto*" in Brazil and at Imola.

merit table . . . I think I could do so. The engine for this car was made here. The propulsion unit is the work of Sig. His, who is a very thorough man when it comes to power output. Then there is Migeod, who looks after th wind tunnel. And Postlethwaite, who collates the

Alboreto's accident during practice for the Monaco Grand Prix was responsible for the 95's return to the track. Berger came fourth with this car. After Monaco, the 95 did not appear any more among the cars assigned to the drivers, not even as a reserve car. It showed up again in Spain, at Saturday practice, with Berger driving. This was the last time it appeared.

Engine: mid-rear 90° V-6. Displacement: 1496,4 cc. Bore and stroke: 81x48,4 mm. Compression ratio: 8:1. Power: 880 bhp at 11.500 rpm (racing), 930 bhp at 11.500 rpm (testing). Valve gear: 4 valves per cylinder, dohc. Fuel system: 2 lateral Garrett turbos, Weber-Marelli electronic digital injection, double injectors. Ignition: single plug, Magneti Marelli electrostatic ignition. Gearbox: 6 speeds + reverse, overhanging longitudinal rear. Brakes: ventilated carbon discs (outboard), Brembo calipers. Frame: monocoque in composite materials (Kevlar and carbon fibre). Suspension, front: unequal length A-arms, pull-rod suspension control. Suspension, rear: twin wishbones, pull-rod suspension control. Tracks: 1791 mm (front), 1673 mm (rear). Wheelbase: 2800 mm. Weight: 542 kg (dry).